Air Fryer Cookbook For Two

The Complete Air Fryer Cookbook – Amazingly Delicious,

Easy, and Healthy Air Fryer Recipes For Two

Table of Contents

Introduction 8

What is an Air Fryer? 10

Benefits 10

How do you use it? 12

Why use it? 17

Air Fryer Recipes for Two 18

Meat 19

Air Fryer Steak 19

Kid-friendly Pigs in a Blanket 20

Philly Cheesesteaks 21

Party Meatballs for Two 22

Fried Pork Chops 23

Beef Jerky..24

Boneless Breaded Pork Chops 25

Hamburgers for Two 26

Country Air-Fried Steak 27

Air Fried Meatloaf..28

Meatloaf Reboot..29

Chinese Style Sweet and Sour Pork 30

Steak Bites..31

Air Fried Roast Beef...32

Beef Fried Rice...33

Air Fried Bacon..34

Hot Dogs 35

Risotto Balls with Peas and Sausage 36

Poultry 37

Mock KFC Chicken Strips 37

Bacon Wrapped Chicken 39

Fried Chicken 40

Rotisserie Chicken 41

Turkey and Cheese Calzone 42

Chicken and Mushroom Kebabs..43

Sweet and Tangy Chicken Wings.. 44

Barbeque Chicken 45

Cornish Game Hens 46

Sriacha Chicken Wings 47

Fried Chicken Wontons 48

Chicken Parmesan with Sauce.. 49

Chicken Croquettes.. 50

Chicken Tenders 51

Seafood 52

Maryland Crab Cakes...52

Fried Fish and Chips...54

Old Fashioned Fish Fry..55

Air Fried Shrimp 56

Air Fried Cod Sandwiches 57

Tuna Cakes..58

Cajun Shrimp Fry...59

Air Fried Salmon 60

Fish Tacos 61

Blackened Shrimp...62

Air Fried Tilapia 63

Fish Nuggets 64

Air Fried Scallops..65

Shrimp Scampi..66

Vegan & Vegetarian..67

Roasted Corn..67

Stuffed Banana Peppers..68

Air Fried Pita Pizza..69

Cauliflower Rice..70

Kale Chips..71

Tofu Scramble..72

Jalapeno Peppers...73

Air Fried Ravioli..74

Sweet Potato Fries...75

Fried Brussels Sprouts...76

Grilled Tomatoes...77

Air Fried Baked Potatoes...78

Air Fried Rice Balls...79

Chinese Orange Tofu..80

Fried Falafel..81

Jicama Fries...82

Fried Artichoke Hearts...83

Avocado Fries..84

Pasta Chips..85

Fried Tortilla Chips...86

Breakfast...87

Hard Boiled Eggs...87

French Toast Bites...88

Home Fried Potatoes..89

Cinnamon Rolls...90

Breakfast Frittata 91

Blueberry Muffins 92

Bran and Apple Muffins 93

Breakfast Pockets 94

Monkey Bread 95

Breakfast Burritos 96

Air Fried Sausage 97

Breakfast Soufflé 98

Bagels 99

Ham and Egg Cups 100

Donut Holes 101

Appetizers 102

Buffalo Fried Cauliflower 102

Air Fried Onion Rings 103

Fried Mozzarella Sticks 104

Fried Pickles 105

Buffalo Wings 106

Jalapeno Poppers 107

Potato Chips 108

Fried Vegetable Tots 109

Blooming Onion Blossom 110

Curly Fries 111

Garlic Bread and Cheese 112

Fried Zucchini Spears 113

Coconut Shrimp 114

Desserts 115

Chocolate Cake 115

Funnel Cake Bites 117

Fried Apple Pie 118

Crustless Coconut pie 119

Apple Chips...120

Fruity Mug Cakes..121

Rainbow Donuts 122

Lemon Pound Cake... 123

Apple Dumplings 124

Chocolate Soufflé 125

Caramel Cheesecake 126

Lemony Cupcakes 127

Mince Pies 128

Banana Bread.. 129

Chocolate Chip Cookies a la Air Fryer 130

Banana S'mores 131

Conclusion.. 132

INTRODUCTION

Imagine, 50 years ago, there was a very small number of ways to cook a meal: on the stove, in the oven or outside on a grill.

Then, in the mid-80s, the microwave started to pop up more and more frequently in homes. Although they had been available for decades, they really didn't catch on and become popular until this time.

From then, technology continued to move forward and different appliances made their debut, offering a variety of cooking alternatives, from the indoor grill to the instant pot, a multi-functioning appliance that prepares food with a variety of methods from slow cooking to high-speed pressure cooking.

With the advent of great new gadgets have been some duds, too. For example, the electric egg poacher seemed like a good idea, but it really didn't do too much to increase efficiencies or ease when poaching eggs. The sandwich grill and the countertop rotisserie were fun... until the cooking was over and you had to clean the thing. What good is it to try to save time when you spent half he night cleaning up?

Yet, the air fryer has proven to be a fantastic investment for people who want to make changes in their cooking styles or are moving toward a healthier lifestyle.

Designed to produce a very similar outcome to fried food, but by using superheated air instead of oil, the air fryer proudly stands on the counter of countless kitchens... instead of gathering dust in the Cabinet of Forgotten Appliances.

With a somewhat limited cooking basket, the air fryer is particularly great for two people, which is why the recipes in this cookbook have been adjusted for two diners... although chances are, there are going to be recipes that you'll want to double, just so you can have them for leftovers.

And when do want to expand a recipe? No problem; the air fryer maintains its temperature so well that it's easy to not only do a second batch of cooking while one is keeping warm in the oven, but it also brings those foods up to temperature quickly when it's time to eat.

Whether you're new to air frying or are looking to expand your air frying recipe collection, we hope you enjoy this collection of air frying recipes for two.

What is an Air Fryer?

What exactly is an air fryer, you ask.

An air fryer is a countertop appliance that uses a fan to move heated air at a rapid speed. It brings into effect a concept known as the Maillard Effect, which is a chemical reaction between reducing sugars and amino acids.

Chemistry lesson aside, the Maillard Effect is what makes cookies a delicious crispy brown, gives seared steaks the incomparable outer 'crust' and roasted coffee the end result that makes it the first part of many people's mornings.

As you can see, the concept has been around for a very, very long time, much longer than Maillard's published findings in 1912.

The air fryer's claim to fame, so to speak, is not the cool chemical reaction, but the fact that it delivers the taste and texture of fried foods with anywhere from an average of 75 percent less oil than traditional oil fried methods.

A light spray of oil on the prepared food, and the air fryer takes care of the rest.

Not all air fryers are created alike, though. There are different cooking capacities and different wattage, which can impact the cooking times. But, just like getting a new pair of shoes, there might be a bit of adjustment needed, which is well worth it in the end.

Benefits

There are a number of different advantages to using an air fryer, from health factors to other practical benefits.

Low fat cooking

The most apparent benefit of the air fryer is that it delivers and end product that is very similar to a fried meal, with a much lower fat content. With traditional frying methods, a food is submerged in hot oil to cook it, resulting in that crispy flavor we have come to associate with fried food. While cooking, though, the oil seeps into the food. While delicious, it's inundated with fat.

With the air fryer, recipes match the old-style fried foods with its flavor and texture, but without the fat.

It's safer
While the air fryer does come up to the same temperature as a regular oven, it is so much safer than using the traditional frying method. For one, there is a minute amount of grease, so you don't have to worry about oil splashing or splattering, which can yield dangerous burns.

Also, the air fryer is contained, so there are no open areas to accidentally burn yourself on. The cooking basket slides into the appliance to begin the cooking process, so you have to consciously pull it out in order to access the food (and hot surfaces).

It heats up fast
According to air fryer manufacturers, the air fryer comes up to temperature in about 2 minutes.

Expanding cooking options
An air fryer can serve as an extension of your oven. Ovens are great for cooking and baking but chances are, if you try to cook two things at once that require different temperatures, what do you do?

For example, what if you are cooking boneless ribs in the oven on a 'low and slow' 320-degree heat, but you also want to make French fries to go with them? An oven-cooked French fry is going to require a much higher heat. Without an air fryer, you'd be forced to either cook the French fries at the low temperature, which is going to result in a soggy mess, or cook the ribs at the higher temperature, which could make them horribly tough.

With the air fryer, you can keep your ribs cooking happily at the lower temperature, while popping your fries in the air fryer and cook them at their ideal temperature... and again, with less fat than frying them.

Great in summer
One comment a lot of air fryer users have made is the fact that they don't have to fire up the oven to make a meal on a hot summer day.

A lot of families adjust their meal plans for different temperatures—soups and roasts in the winter and quicker meals with salads in the summer. Still, there are going to be times that a meal would require cooking in the oven. And if it's already 90 degrees outside, it's hard to think about adding to that heat with an oven that is kicking out 350 or more degrees.

Consequently, with the air fryer, you can avoid the oven altogether.

It's portable
No more difficult than loading up a crock pot to take to a pot luck dinner, the air fryer is something that you can pack up easily to lend a hand with cooking at a friend's barbeque or a big family meal at a relative's home.

It's ideal for leftovers
Have you ever gone out to eat but just couldn't finish those fries that came with your meal? You bring them home and then are faced with a huge waste of energy by firing up the oven to heat a handful of once-delicious fries. Or, you pop them in the microwave and pull out a soggy mess.

The air fryer heats up leftovers quickly and easily, virtually restoring your leftovers to the same delicious state they were in the first time around.

It's easy to clean
One of the biggest downfalls for any appliance is ease of cleaning. It might be the newest, fastest appliance in your kitchen, but if it takes longer to clean than it does to actually cook the meal, what are the chance you're going to use it often, if ever?

Once cool, it's easy to wipe down the fryer, and the removable components are safe to put in the dishwasher.

Plus, since there is very little oil, you're going to see the same gelatinous coating that tends to build up on a traditional oil fryer.

As you can see, an air fryer has a tremendous number of benefits. The biggest, of course, is that it creates delicious, low fat 'fried' food, but there are numerous other advantages to the air fryer as well.

How do you use it?
An air fryer is very easy to use.

First, plug it in. Next, use the adjustable temperature gauge to set the temperature, depending on your recipe's instructions.

It isn't absolutely necessary to preheat the air fryer, and you can put the food in prior to turning the fryer on, but it will impact your cooking time on the other end. Unless a recipe specifically says to put the food in a cold air fryer, it makes sense to take that two minutes to preheat the air fryer before you start to cook.

Next, when preparing your food, less is more when you're using oil. It truly takes only a few spritzes of oil in many cases. You'll generally want to spray the basket with a light spray of oil, and then spray a light coating on the food as well. A little bit of oil is important because it helps with the resulting 'fried' taste and texture.

The frying basket is designed to allow the excess oil to drip down and away from the food, which will be collected in a drip tray directly under the frying basket.

While cooking your food, it's recommended that you give the frying basket a good shake every now and then to make sure the oils are evenly distributed. Also, some recipes require turning over the food at some point through the cooking process, so it's useful to note that although it's a lot more hands off than traditional frying, for example, this is not a 'turn it on and go walk the dog' type of cooking.

Toward the end of a recipe, it's important to watch for overcooking. Again, since every air fryer is different, some recipes may need to be adapted for your particular style and model.

The frying basket is often attached to the cooking drawer. Before you turn the basket upside down to remove the cooked food, make sure it is unlocked from the drawer... and the drip pan.

Besides the basic instructions, there are some other handy tips to keep in mind:
1. Generally speaking, you can adapt your favorite recipes to the air fryer. Because of the different cooking method, a good rule of thumb is to set the temperature on your air fryer to about 25 degrees lower than a traditional oven setting. Also, start checking for doneness about 10 to 15 minutes before the original recipe cooking time.
2. Give the air fryer plenty of space. Don't forget, even though the air fryer is compact, it is going to kick out some hot air. When using the air fryer, make sure there is plenty of room between the back (where the exhaust fan is located) and any walls or other obstructions.

3. Check in often. Unlike a traditional oven where excessive 'peeking' may impact the cooking time since the oven has to come back up to temperature, the air fryer heats up quickly. So, don't be bashful about checking in often to monitor progress, particularly as you're getting used to this cooking style.

4. Invest in a good oil spray bottle. Since this process uses a small amount of oil, it's a waste to brush on the oil. When you use your own hand-pump spray bottle, you can not only use your preferred oil, but it is more natural than using an aerosol-propelled cooking spray.

5. Don't overcrowd the cooking basket. The air fryer works by circulating the air around the cooking food, so if you overfill the basket, the appliance isn't going to be able to do its job as effectively

6. Consider accessories. You can use any ovenproof dish or pan in the airpot, but make sure it doesn't touch the heating element or crowd the cooking basket too much. There are a number of accessories designed specifically for the air fryer, if your model doesn't already come with accessories.

7. Add a little water to the drip tray when you're cooking with fatty foods. This will help the dripping oil from smoking as the air fryer is cooking.

8. Coat your foods with one thing in mind: air. Lightly breading a food or adding bread crumbs to a batter might not hold up to the air fryer. The very principle of the air fryer can wreak havoc on a halfhearted breading, because it's apt to just blow the bread crumbs off of the food. Instead, as you are breading your foods, don't hold back on pressing your bread crumbs into the batter.

It's always useful to have some estimated cooking times on hand, so this chart will likely be a good starting point to keep on hand.

Type	Food	Cooking Time	Temperature (Fahrenheit)
Fish	Breaded shrimp	9 minutes	400
Fish	Fish fillet	10 - 12 minutes	380-400
Fish	Frozen fish fillets	14 minutes	400
Fish	Frozen fish sticks	10 minutes	400
Fish	Scallops	5 - 7 minutes	400
Fish	Shrimp	6 minutes	400
Meat	Bacon	5 - 7 minutes	400

Meat	Beef roast	45 - 55 minutes	390
Meat	Chicken Breast, boneless	12 minutes	380
Meat	Chicken Breast, with bones	28 minutes	370
Meat	Chicken drumsticks	20 minutes	370
Meat	Chicken nuggets	12 minutes	390
Meat	Chicken tenders	8 - 10 minutes	360
Meat	Chicken Thighs, boneless	18 minutes	380
Meat	Chicken Thighs, with bones	22 minutes	380
Meat	Chicken wings	12 minutes	400
Meat	Filet mignon	18 minutes	400
Meat	Flank steak	12 minutes	400
Meat	Game hen	20 minutes	390
Meat	Hamburger	18 - 20 minutes	370
Meat	Lamb chops	8 - 12 minutes	400
Meat	London broil	20 - 28 minutes	400
Meat	Meatballs	7 minutes	380
Meat	Pork Chops, bone in	12 minutes	400
Meat	Pork loin	50 - 55 minutes	360
Meat	Pork tenderloin	15 minutes	370
Meat	Rack of lamb	22 minutes	380
Meat	Sausage	15 minutes	380
Meat	T-Bone steak	10 - 15 minutes	400
Meat	Whole chicken	75 minutes	360
Sides	Mozzarella sticks	8 minutes	400
Sides	Onion rings	8 minutes	400
Sides	Thick french fries	19 minutes	390
Sides	Thin french fries	15 minutes	390
Vegetable	Asparagus	5 minutes	400
Vegetable	Beets	40 minutes	400

Vegetable	Broccoli	6 minutes	400
Vegetable	Brussels sprouts	15 minutes	380
Vegetable	Carrots	15 minutes	380
Vegetable	Cauliflower	12 minutes	400
Vegetable	Com on the cob	6 minutes	390
Vegetable	Eggplant	15 minutes	400
Vegetable	Fennel	15 minutes	370
Vegetable	Green beans	5 minutes	400
Vegetable	Kale	12 minutes	250
Vegetable	Mushrooms	7 minutes	400
Vegetable	Onions	10 minutes	400
Vegetable	Peppers	15 minutes	400
Vegetable	Potatoes, baby	15 minutes	400
Vegetable	Potatoes, whole	40 minutes	400
Vegetable	Squash	12 minutes	400
Vegetable	Sweet potato	30 minutes	380
Vegetable	Tomatoes	10 minutes	180
Vegetable	Zucchini	12 minutes	350

While there is no question that the air fryer is an amazing piece of machinery, it is important to keep a few things in mind.

Just like the cup of coffee that you get at your favorite coffee shop or fast food joint, the air fryer carries the caution that it does yield hot foods. It is somewhat easy to forget, though, because it's hard to believe that a small appliance like this can pack such a punch.

Plus, it heats up so quickly that it might be assumed that it will cool down just as rapidly. The air fryer will maintain a level of heat for quite a while, and you should always exercise caution when removing the fryer basket and the food. It will be extremely hot.

As with any cooking appliance, don't leave the air fryer unattended while in use. While the safety features on modern appliances have come a long way, Murphy's Law is always looking for a way to wreak havoc. Plus, you've worked hard to make that meal—why take the chance of going for a walk and having your dinner be burnt to a crisp because you accidentally set the temperature too high or got to swapping stories with your neighbor and lost track of time?

Also, while the inserts are dishwasher safe, you should never submerge the air fryer in water. The elements and other components should not come in contact with water or cleaning sprays, or it might impact the way the air fryer operates.
Finally, when not in use, it's a good idea to unplug your air fryer.

Why use it?

The air fryer is one of the most useful products on the market today for your kitchen. Of course, quality that initially attracts most people to an air fryer is the promise of a lower fat alternative to the traditional fried food fare.

Health benefits aside, the air fryer offers a quality meal with the convenience of lower cooking times and uncomplicated instructions.

It's time to update your kitchen appliances and bring in the air fryer. The proof isn't necessarily in the pudding (although I'm sure there's a way to make it work!) but in the French fries... the great equalizer of all fried foods.

When shopping for an air fryer, keep capacity in mind. One rather common complaint, especially when air fryers were first being developed, was that the capacity was too small, so it was too hard to cook a full meal.

As a rule of thumb, fryers that are 1 to 2 quarts in size are good for cooking snacks and heating up leftovers. A fryer that is 2.2 to 3 quarts are ideal for a household with one to two people, while one that is 5.3 to 5.8 quarts in size are good for larger families with 3 to 5 members.

You can go up to 16 quart sized fryers for super large families, cooking full sized meals (like a whole pizza or a turkey) or for bulk cooking.

Regardless, think about your cooking needs and number of people you might cook for and make your purchase accordingly.

We hope you enjoy the recipes in the following guide so you can cook your way to a healthier you!

Air Fryer Recipes for Two

What is the benefit of a cookbook for two?

According to statista.com, a website combining information from more than twenty-two thousand sources, the average number of household members is on a gradual decline. In 2017, the average number of people in one household is 2.54. This means that there is are many two-member households in our country.

This demographic may be newlyweds, single parent households, or empty nesters. Of course, households expand when kids are in the house, but with children going off to college at 17 or 18, it really is a short amount of time that there are going to be kids in the house, generally speaking.

Consequently, a traditional cookbook may not work for smaller households. Cooking too much not only puts unnecessary strain on food budgets, but it also means a ton of leftovers to contend with. And if your family doesn't eat leftovers? That extra food goes into the garbage.

This cookbook takes the guesswork out of having to cut ingredients and estimated cooking times down to accommodate the dual member household.

From appetizers to hearty dishes to desserts, the Air Fryer Cookbook For Two serves up delicious healthier alternatives to traditional fried foods, while being kind to your food budget and limited time.

Meat

Air frying is a fantastic, low fat alternative for any battered, fried meat, but don't limit yourself to thinking that air frying is all about a heavy breaded food. Almost any protein-packed meal can be modified to be used in an air fryer, from roast beef to meatballs. Air fryers also make a mean steak, whether it's a rib-eye or a chicken fried steak with all the trimmings.

Air Fryer Steak

This simple recipe can be used with any other type of grilling steak, with or without seasoning variations.

Prep time: 2 minutes
Cook time: 6 minutes
Serves: 2

Ingredients:
- 2 New York Strip Steaks
- 1 Tbsp. Worcestershire Sauce
- Salt and Pepper to Taste

Instructions:
1. Rub salt and pepper on steaks, and drizzle Worcestershire sauce on both sides.
2. Heat your air fryer to 400 degrees for 6 minutes.
3. Place the steaks in the air fryer. Set the timer for 12 minutes, flipping after about 6 minutes to ensure even cooking. For a rare steak, the internal temperature should be 130-140 degrees; medium rare, 145 degrees; medium, 160 degrees or well done 170 degrees. Adjust your cooking time appropriately.
4. Serve.

Kid-friendly Pigs in a Blanket

Ever feel like taking a break from the traditional 'grown up' meal? These are quick and easy... and a great way to pay homage to your inner child.

Prep time: 5 minutes
Cook time: 8 minutes
Serves: 2

Ingredients:
- 1 can refrigerated crescent rolls
- 1 package of cocktail franks

Instructions:
1. Drain cocktail franks for the package, then pat 16 franks dry with a paper towel.
2. Remove crescent rolls from the package, unrolling them into flat triangles. Cut each triangle in half, lengthwise.
3. Roll one cocktail frank into each of the triangle halves.
4. Heat your air fryer to 330 degrees for 6 minutes. Add half of the rolls in the frying basket and fry for about 7-8 minutes. Remove and repeat process for the remaining rolls.
5. Serve.

Philly Cheesesteaks

This is a quick, easy meal for after a long day at work and easy to adjust to different taste preferences.

Prep time: 10 minutes
Cook time: 20 minutes
Serves: 2

Ingredients:
- 2 bulky rolls
- ½ lb. shaved steak
- 2/3 cup shredded mozzarella cheese
- 1 onion, sliced
- 1 Tbsp. Worcestershire sauce
- 1 green pepper, sliced
- ½ cup mushrooms

Instructions:
1. Heat air fryer to 360 degrees.
2. Put onion and green pepper slices in air fryer basket. Spritz with olive oil and cook for about 10 minutes. Remove and set side.
3. With a fork, separate the shaved steak. Drizzle the Worcestershire sauce on the meat and add it to the frying bowl. Fry at 360 degrees for 5 to 6 minutes, mixing up with a fork every few minutes to ensure an even cook.
4. Return the green pepper and onion to the frying bowl, stirring in with the beef. Top with cheese and cook for about 3 to 4 more minutes.
5. Remove from air fryer, put in rolls and serve.

Party Meatballs for Two

This recipe serves two as a meal, but you could easily double it and serve as cocktail meatballs, or triple the recipe and bring them to a potluck.

Prep time: 5 minutes
Cook time: 15 minutes
Serves: 2

Ingredients:
- ½ lb. ground beef
- 1 gingersnap cookie
- 2/3 cup ketchup
- 1 Tbsp. Worcestershire sauce
- Dash of Tabasco
- Dash of lemon juice
- ¼ cup brown sugar
- ¼ Tbsp. dry yellow mustard

Instructions:
1. Allow ground beef to sit on the counter for about 10 minutes before making your meatballs. Crush your cookie and combine it with the ground beef. In a separate bowl, combine remaining ingredients, stirring well. Add to the beef mixture, and use your hands to thoroughly combine all the ingredients.
2. Heat your air fryer to 375 degrees. Add meatballs and air fry for about 15 minutes. These are great with a pasta sauce with spaghetti or in a sweet and sour sauce over rice.

Fried Pork Chops

If you want to make these extra crispy, spray them with a little cooking spray before putting them in the air fryer.

Prep time: 5 minutes
Cook time: 24 minutes
Serves: 2

Ingredients:

- 2 bone in pork chops, about ¾ inch in thickness
- 3 Tbsp. Dijon mustard
- ½ cup bread crumbs
- ½ tsp. smoked paprika
- Salt and pepper to taste

Instructions:

1. Heat your air fryer to 400 degrees.
2. Coat your pork chops with mustard and set aside.
3. In a bowl, thoroughly mix your seasonings with the bread crumbs. Press coated pork chops into the bread crumb mixture.
4. Air fry for 12 minutes, then flip and cook for another 12 minutes.

Beef Jerky

The biggest downside to cooking beef jerky with a dehydrator is having to smell it all day without being able to sample it. Now, with the air fryer, you can cook a batch in an hour! Perfect for taking on a hike or as a protein-packed snack between meals.

Prep time: 35 minutes
Rest time: Refrigerate overnight
Cook time: 12 minutes
Serves: 2

Ingredients:
- 1 lb. lean beef (a London broil or equivalent)
- 1 Tbsp. liquid smoke
- 2/3 cup brown sugar
- 1 Tbsp. olive oil
- 2 Tbsp. Montreal Steak Seasoning
- 2 Tbsp. Worcestershire sauce

Instructions:
1. Place steak in the freezer for about 15 to 20 minutes to partially freeze. This makes it a lot easier to cut thin slices, which is key for good jerky. After the meat is partially frozen, use a sharp knife to cut the meat against the bias (against the grain).
2. Combine the remaining ingredients in a plastic storage bag that can zip lock closed. When the ingredients are well mixed, add the slices of meat. Press as much air as you can out of the bag and seal it shut.
3. Put the bag in the refrigerator to marinade the meat, tossing the contents around occasionally to ensure a consistent marinade.
4. After the meat is marinated to desired length of time, remove from the refrigerator.
5. Preheat the air fryer to 350 degrees. Line the rack with aluminum foil and place a layer of beef on the bottom of the fryer. Depending on the size of your fryer, you may need to cook in two batches so you don't overcrowd the fryer.
6. Cook for 45 minutes, then flip over and cook for an additional 15 minutes, testing for doneness.

Boneless Breaded Pork Chops

These are delicious served up with a dish of homemade applesauce to dunk in!

Prep time: 3 minutes
Cook time: 12 minutes
Serves: 2

Ingredients:
- Cooking spray
- 2 boneless pork chops, about ¾ inch thick
- 1 egg
- ¼ cup panko bread crumbs
- ¼ cup cornflakes
- 1 Tbsp. Parmesan cheese
- ½ tsp. smoked paprika
- ¼ tsp. garlic powder
- ¼ tsp. onion powder
- Kosher salt
- Dash of pepper

Directions:
1. Heat your air fryer to 400 degrees. Spray your basket with cooking oil, preferably olive oil.
2. Press kosher salt into both sides of the pork chops, set aside.
3. In a bowl, beat the egg. Dip the pork chops into the beaten egg and set aside.
4. In another bowl, crush the cornflakes. Add the bred crumbs, cheese, paprika, garlic and onion powders, and salt and pepper to taste. Combine well. Press the crumb mixture onto both sides of the pork chops.
5. Add the pork chops to the air fryer, spraying the top lightly with a coating of cooking oil.
6. Cook for 6 minutes. Turn and cook for another 12 minutes.

Hamburgers for Two

Once you've tried cooking a hamburger with an air fryer, there is no going back to other methods.

Prep time: 10 minutes
Cook time: 10 minutes
Serves: 2

Ingredients:
- ½ lb. ground beef
- 1 Tbsp. Worcestershire sauce
- ¼ tsp. garlic powder
- Salt and pepper to taste

Directions:
1. Heat your air fryer to 350 degrees. If using a low fat ground beef, spray the basket lightly with cooking spray. Skip this step for a fattier ground beef.
2. Combine ground beef with the seasonings. Divide in half and form patties. Drizzle Worcestershire sauce on both sizes.
3. Air fry the burgers for 5 minutes. Flip and cook for another 5 minutes for a medium done burger.

Country Air-Fried Steak

This southern influenced comfort food is (somewhat) better for you now, with the introduction of the air fryer!

Prep time: 10 minutes
Cook time: 12 minutes
Serves: 2

Ingredients:
- 2 sirloin steaks, about 6 ounces each
- 6 eggs
- 1 ½ cup flour
- ¾ cup panko bread crumbs
- 2 tsp. garlic salt
- 2 tsp. onion powder
- 2 tsp. pepper
- 8 oz. ground sweet sausage
- ¼ cup flour
- 1 ½ cup milk
- 1 tsp. pepper

Instructions:
1. Heat your air fryer to 370 degrees.
2. Combine garlic salt, onion powder the 2 teaspoons of pepper and the panko bread crumbs.
3. Pound the steaks so they are thin. Press steaks into the 1 ½ cups of flour, then in the egg, and then in the bread crumb mixture.
4. Put the steak in the airpot and fry for 12 minutes. If you have a smaller fryer, you'll need to cook these one at a time so they aren't crowded.
5. While the steaks are cooking, cook the sausage in a pan over medium heat. Drain fat. Add the ¼ cup of flour and mix well until the flour and sausage is combined. Slowly add milk and stir until thickened, cooking for about three minutes.
6. When steaks are ready, plate them and drizzle the sausage gravy over the top. Serve.

Air Fried Meatloaf

If you don't like the texture of onion in your meatloaf, you could eliminate the salt and onion and use a half packet of onion soup mix instead.

Prep time: 5 minutes
Cook time: 20 minutes
Serves: 2

Ingredients:
- ½ lb. ground beef
- ½ lb. ground turkey
- 1 onion, chopped
- ¼ cup panko bread crumbs
- 3 Tbsp. ketchup
- ¼ cup brown sugar
- 1 egg, beaten
- Salt and pepper to taste

Instructions:
1. Preheat air fryer to 400 degrees.
2. Let the ground beef and ground turkey sit on the counter for 10 to 15 minutes, as it will be easier to hand mix without being chilled from the refrigerator.
3. Combine all the ingredients.
4. Form into a loaf in a dish and place the dish in the frying basket. Spritz the top with a little olive oil.
5. Bake for 25 minutes, or until well browned. Let settle for about 10 minutes before serving.

Meatloaf Reboot

If you are like millions of others that love leftover meatloaf, this recipe will take that devotion to a whole new level. Fry these up and enjoy as leftovers with a few sides, or as one of the most delicious sandwiches ever!

Prep time: 5 minutes
Cook time: 9 minutes
Serves: 2

Ingredients:
1. 4 slices of leftover meatloaf, cut about 1-inch thick.
2. Instructions:
3. Preheat your air fryer to 350 degrees.
4. Spray each side of the meatloaf slices with cooking spray. Add the slices to the air fryer and cook for about 9 to 10 minutes. Don't turn the slices halfway through the cooking cycle, because they may break apart. Instead, keep them on one side to cook to ensure they stay together.

Chinese Style Sweet and Sour Pork

Try this great, low fat twist on the favorite flavors on your Chinese meal menu.

Prep time: 15 minutes
Cook time: 12 minutes
Serves: 2

Ingredients:
- 1 lb. pork tenderloin, cut into chunks
- 1 egg
- ½ tsp. sesame oil
- ½ cup cornstarch
- Dash of Chinese Five Spice
- 1 tsp. canola oil

For the sauce:
- ¼ cup brown sugar
- 3 Tbsp. ketchup
- ¼ cup rice vinegar
- 2 tsp. soy sauce
- ¼ tsp. garlic salt

Instructions:
1. Preheat the air fryer to 340 degrees
2. In a bowl, combine cornstarch, Chinese Five Spice and salt and pepper to taste. In a separate bowl, beat the egg with the sesame oil.
3. Coat the pieces of pork in the cornstarch mixture, shaking off any excess. Then dip into egg mixture, and back into the cornstarch.
4. Spritz oil on the air fryer basket. Add the pork and add a little extra oil sprays. Cook for 8 to 12 minutes.
5. In the meantime, prepare the sweet and sour sauce by combining the brown sugar, ketchup, soy sauce, garlic salt and vinegar in a small saucepan. Whisk thoroughly over medium heat and simmer for about 5 minutes.
6. When the pork is cooked thoroughly, remove from the air fryer and mix in the sauce. Serve.

Steak Bites

Prep time: 5 minutes
Cook time: 9 minutes
Serves: 2

Ingredients:

- 1 lb. London broil steak
- ¼ cup soy sauce
- 3 Tbsp. Worcestershire sauce
- 2 Tbsp. lemon juice
- 1 Tbsp. garlic salt
- 1 Tbsp. onion powder
- 1 tsp. pepper, ground
- 2 eggs, beaten
- 1 cup flour
- 1/3 cup Parmesan cheese
- Salt and pepper to taste

Instructions:

1. Cut the steak into 6 even pieces. Combine soy sauce, Worcestershire sauce, lemon juice, garlic salt, onion powder and ground pepper to a plastic zippered storage bag. Seal and shake vigorously to combine well. Drop in the steak pieces. Press out as much air as possible and seal.
2. Put in the refrigerator and allow to marinade for at least 12-16 hours, giving it a good shake every now and then to redistribute the flavoring.
3. When you are ready to cook, heat the air fryer to 350 degrees.
4. In a dish, combine the flour, Parmesan cheese and salt and pepper. Set aside. Beat the two eggs in another bowl and set aside. Remove the steak pieces from the bag and pat dry with a paper towel.
5. Next, dredge the steak pieces, one at a time, in the egg, and then the flour mixture. Set aside. Repeat the process with the remaining steak bites.
6. Pray cooking spray on the frying rack and add the steak pieces. Cook for 10 minutes, then carefully flip them over and cook for an additional 10 minutes.

Air Fried Roast Beef

This recipe will yield leftovers, perfect for lunch the next day!

Prep time: 10 minutes
Cook time: 55 minutes
Serves: 2

Ingredients:
- Pot roast, about 3 pounds
- 8 small round potatoes
- 2 Tbsp. olive oil
- 1 tsp. dried rosemary, divided
- 1/3 tsp. thyme
- Salt and pepper to taste

Instructions:
1. Heat the air fryer to 360 degrees.
2. Take about 1 Tbsp. of the olive oil and rub it over the beef. Then, mix together about ½ tsp. of the rosemary, the thyme and salt and pepper. Rub the spices over the beef, making sure to coat all the sides. Place the roast in the fryer basket and cook for about 15 minutes.
3. In the meantime, cut the potatoes in half. Take the remaining olive oil and toss the potatoes in the oil with the other half teaspoon of rosemary, along with a little salt and pepper. Set aside.
4. When the time is up, flip the roast over and add the potatoes to the basket. Cook for an additional 10 minutes. Then give the basket a good shake, rotate the roast a bit in the basket and cook for 10 more minutes.
5. Check the roast and remove when it is at the level of doneness that you prefer.
6. When cooked to satisfaction, remove the roast, cover with aluminum foil and allow to rest without cutting.
7. While the roast is resting, air fry the potatoes for an additional 6 to 8 minutes, giving the basket a good shake every so often.
8. When the potatoes are done, remove. Slice the roast and serve with the potatoes.

Beef Fried Rice

This recipe calls for cooked beef, so you can either use leftover roast, or roast beef from the deli—they are more than happy to slice thick slices as opposed to slicing thin for sandwiches.

Prep time: 5 minutes
Cook time: 20 minutes
Serves: 2

Ingredients:
- ¾ cup roast beef, or other precooked beef, diced in small cubes
- 1 tsp. sesame oil
- 2 cup white rice, precooked
- 2/3 cup petite peas, frozen
- ½ tsp. oyster sauce
- 5 Tbsp. soy sauce
- ½ onion, diced
- 1 scrambled egg, precooked

Instructions:
1. Heat air fryer to 360 degrees.
2. Put the cooked rice in a bowl. Add the sesame oil, soy sauce and the oyster sauce and mix well.
3. Next, add the onion and mix again.
4. Put the mixture into a pan that will fit in your air fryer and place the pan in the fryer basket.
5. Cook for about 17 minutes. Add the peas and scrambled egg to the rice mixture and stir well. Air fry for an additional three minutes.
6. Stir again and serve.

Air Fried Bacon

This is one of the easiest ways to make bacon, without the splattering or a lot of cleanup needed. Add a little water to the drip pan to help keep the fat from smoking while the bacon is cooking.

Prep time: 1 minute
Cook time: 10 minutes
Serves: 2

Ingredients:
- 6 to 10 strips of bacon

Instructions:
1. Heat Oven to 350 degrees.
2. Lay the bacon in a single layer in the fryer basket. Fry for about 5 minutes, then give the basket a good shake. Fry for another 3 to 5 minutes, depending on the amount of bacon cooked.

Hot Dogs

If you're in the New England area, this recipe is fantastic using red hot dogs. Regardless of your preference though—traditional brown hot dogs or cheese stuffed dogs—this recipe is sure to please.

Prep time: 2 minutes
Cook time: 9 minutes
Serves: 2

Ingredients:

- 2 hot dogs, any variety
- 2 hot dog buns

Instructions:

1. Heat your air fryer to 390 degrees. First, spray your hot dog buns lightly with a cooking spray and add to the cooking tray. Air fry for about 2 minutes on one side, then flip the bun over and fry for another2 minutes.
2. Carefully remove buns and set aside. Add the hot dogs to the air fryer and fry for about 5 minutes. If you want, you can add cheese and cook for an additional two minutes.
3. Remove hot dogs, add to buns and serve.

Risotto Balls with Peas and Sausage

Prep time: 4 minutes
Cook time: 8 minutes
Serves: 2

Ingredients:
- ½ cup peas
- ½ cup cooked ground sweet sausage, strained well
- 1 ½ cup chilled risotto
- 2 large eggs
- 1 ¾ cup panko bread crumbs
- ¾ cup flour

Instructions:
1. Heat air fryer to 350 degrees.
2. Scramble the eggs in one small bowl. Add flour to a second bowl and panko bread crumbs to the third.
3. Combine risotto, sausage and peas carefully. Take 1 tablespoon of the risotto mixture and roll into a ball. Repeat with remaining risotto mixture.
4. Coat each ball with flour. Then roll in egg scramble and coat in the panko bread crumbs.
5. Carefully place the risotto balls in the air fryer. Cook for 5-8 minutes until they are crispy. Serve immediately.

Poultry

While you can cook just about anything in an air fryer, with this appliance, you can really explore those breaded recipes you've wanted to try but shied away from because of the fat content they would yield in a traditional fried food recipe.

So, have fun and dive into a plate of fried chicken without the guilt. Or get your fingers sticky with the delicious barbeque chicken, courtesy of your air fryer.

Mock KFC Chicken Strips

This recipe is all the flavor of the popular fast food chicken strips, but without the extra fat from a traditional oil fryer! The spice mix ingredients make a whole batch which can stored for later use. You can reduce the quantities as necessary, since about one tablespoon is needed for this recipe.

Prep time: 5 minutes
Cook time: 12 minutes
Serves: 2

Ingredients:
For the spice mix (this makes a whole batch which can stored for later use, but can be reduced as necessary, as about one tablespoon is needed for this recipe):
- 2 Tbsp. smoked paprika
- 1 Tbsp. parsley
- 1 Tbsp. dried chives
- 1 Tbsp. oregano
- 2 tsp. dried thyme
- 2 tsp. cayenne pepper
- 1 Tbsp. tarragon
- 1 tsp. garlic salt
- 1 tsp. onion salt
- ½ tsp. pepper

For the recipe:
- 1 boneless skinless chicken breast
- ¼ cup flour
- 1 Tbsp. rolled oats
- 1 Tbsp. coconut, unsweetened

- 1 egg, beaten
- ½ cup bread crumbs, unflavored

Instructions:

1. Combine the spice mix. Reserve about 1 tablespoon and store the rest for future use.
2. Heat air fryer to 350 degrees. In a bowl, combine one tablespoon of spice blend, coconut, oats and unseasoned bread crumbs. In second bowl, scramble your egg. In the third bowl, add the flour.
3. Cut your chicken breast into even strips. Coat the strips in the flour and then dredge in the egg. Finally, coat the chicken with the spice mixture.
4. Add the chicken strips to the air fryer. Fry for 8 minutes. Reduce the temperature to 320 degrees and cook for another 4 minutes. Serve hot.

Bacon Wrapped Chicken

A small layer of cream cheese with the bacon turns this chicken recipe into a delicious meal.

Prep time: 8 minutes
Cook time: 15 minutes
Serves: 2

Ingredients:
- 6 strips bacon, cut in half
- 2 boneless skinless chicken breasts
- 2 Tbsp. cream cheese

Instructions:
1. Preheat air fryer to 350 degrees
2. Cut the chicken breasts into 12 even pieces. Spread out the bacon strips ad spread them with the cream cheese.
3. Put chicken on the cheese-coated bacon strips and roll so that the cheese is touching the chicken and the bacon forms the outer layer. Secure with a toothpick.
4. Place chicken in the preheated air fryer. Cook for 15 minutes.

Fried Chicken

Who doesn't love fried chicken? Now you can have all the flavor with less fat!

Prep time: 4 minutes
Cook time: 25 minutes
Serves: 2

Ingredients:

- 4 chicken thighs, skin trimmed
- 2/3 cup flour
- 2 Tbsp. Old Bay Seasoning
- 1 tsp. seasoned salt
- 1 egg

Instructions:

1. Preheat your air fryer to 400 degrees.
2. Combine Old Bay seasoning with the flour and salt. Set aside. In a separate bowl, scramble your egg.
3. Press the chicken thighs into the flour mixture. Then dip in the beaten egg and dip into the flour mixture again.
4. Add the coated chicken pieces to the air fryer. Reduce temperature to 350 degrees and cook for 25 minutes.

Rotisserie Chicken

A whole chicken is a lot of meat for two people, but the leftovers are so delicious in for sandwiches.

Prep time: 4 minutes
Cook time: 25 minutes
Serves: 2

Ingredients:
- 1 whole fryer chicken, 3-4 pounds
- 2 Tbsp. olive oil
- 2 tsp. seasoning salt
- ¼ tsp. garlic powder
- ¼ tsp. onion powder
- 1/8 tsp. turmeric
- Pinch of cornstarch

Instructions:
1. Preheat the air fryer to 350 degrees.
2. Combine the seasoning salt, garlic powder, onion powder, turmeric and cornstarch. Mix well and set aside.
3. Prepare the chicken by removing any giblets and dry with a paper towel. Rub olive oil onto the chicken and coat with the seasoning.
4. Turn the chicken upside down and place it, breast side down, in the air fryer. Fry for a half hour at 350 degrees. Then flip the chicken over and air fry for another 30 minutes. Remove when internal temperature is 165 degrees. Let chicken rest for 8 to 10 minutes and serve.

Turkey and Cheese Calzone

Have leftover chicken or turkey? Try these calzones to use up some of your precooked meat.

Prep time: 6 minutes
Cook time: 10 minutes
Serves: 2

Ingredients:
- Package of pizza dough
- 2 Tbsp. pizza sauce
- 4 slices bacon, cooked
- 2 cup leftover chicken or turkey shredded
- 1 egg
- 2/3 cup pizza cheese blend
- Salt and pepper to taste
- 1 tsp. oregano

Instructions:
1. Preheat air fryer to 350 degrees
2. Roll out pizza dough to the size of a small pizza. Mix pizza sauce and oregano together, and spoon on the pizza, making sure to leave a good gap at the edges all around.
3. Add your chicken, bacon and cheese, as well as any other preferred toppings on one half of the circle. Be careful not to overload the pizza though.
4. Beat the egg and brush it over the topping layer. Fold over the side without toppings and seal the edges. Brush the top of the calzone with remaining egg.
5. Put in air fryer and cook for about 10 minutes.

Chicken and Mushroom Kebabs

Prep time: 10 minutes
Cook time: 23 minutes
Serves: 2

Ingredients:
- 2 boneless skinless chicken breasts
- ¼ cup honey
- 1/3 cup soy sauce
- 1 Tbsp. sesame seeds
- 2 bell peppers, diced in 1-inch pieces
- 1 cup mushrooms
- 1 summer squash, diced in 1-inch pieces
- Olive oil or other cooking spray
- Salt and pepper to taste

Instructions:
1. Soak bamboo skewers in water and preheat air fryer to 325 degrees.
2. Cut chicken into 1 inch cubes. Spray with oil and season with salt and pepper.
3. Combine honey, sesame seeds and soy sauce, stirring well.
4. Assemble skewers with chicken and cut up vegetables. Coat with the honey sauce and put in the air fryer basket.
5. Air fry for 10 minutes. Brush with honey mixture again and cook for a remaining 5 to 10 minutes.

Sweet and Tangy Chicken Wings

The combination of honey and lemon juice makes for a deliciously tangy addition on chicken wings.

Prep time: 5 minutes
Marinade time: 6 hours to 1 day
Cook time: 9 minutes
Serves: 2

Ingredients:
- 2 Tbsp. honey
- 2 Tbsp. lemon juice
- 2 Tbsp. soy sauce
- Salt and pepper to taste

Ingredients:
1. Rinse wings and pat try with a paper towel. Combing remaining ingredients, stirring well. Add the marinade in a plastic sealable storage bag along with the chicken wings.
2. Let marinade in the refrigerator for at least 6 hours, preferably a full day.
3. When ready to bake, remove the chicken and let them come to room temperature, about a half hour.
4. In the meantime, preheat the air fryer to 350 degrees.
5. Remove chicken from marinade and put in the air fryer. Cook for 6 minutes, and then flip over. Cook for an additional 3 minutes, watching carefully that they don't burn because of they honey in the coating.
6. Serve immediately.

Barbeque Chicken

This is so easy to make, quick to marinade and yields a deliciously gooey, flavorful meal.

Prep time: 40 minutes
Cook time: 15 minutes
Serves: 2

Ingredients:
- 2 chicken breasts, boneless and skinless
- 1/3 cup brown sugar
- 3 Tbsp. balsamic vinegar
- 3 Tbsp. olive oil
- ¼ cup soy sauce
- 2 Tbsp. Dijon mustard

Instructions:
1. Mix all the ingredients but the chicken in a bowl, whisking well. When combined, add the chicken breasts and turn over to coat completely.
2. Cover and place in the refrigerator for at least ½ hour to let marinade.
3. After the chicken has marinated, remove from the refrigerator and turn over again to coat once more.
4. Preheat the air fryer to 380 degrees. Spritz the frying rack with a little cooking spray and add the chicken.
5. Cook for 15 minutes. Serve.

Cornish Game Hens

These are a neat, easy meal for two people. If you want, dress your dinner up with a variety of dipping sauces to choose from.

Prep time: 5 minutes
Cook time: 30 minutes
Serves: 2

Ingredients:
- 2 cup Cornish game hens
- 2 small onions
- 3 Tbsp. olive oil
- 2 tsp. garlic salt
- Salt and pepper to taste

Instructions:
1. Preheat air fryer to 390 degrees.
2. Remove gizzards from the hens. Rub the skin with olive oil.
3. Combine salt, pepper and garlic salt. Rub the mixture over the skin of the hens.
4. Peel the onions and put them in the cavities of the Cornish game hens, and the tie the legs together with kitchen twine.
5. Lightly spray the fryer basket with cooking spray and place the hens in the basket, breast side up.
6. Cook for about 25 minutes. Use a meat thermometer to check the temperature. The hens' internal temperature should reach 170 degrees.
7. When cooked, remove. Allow to sit for about 10 minutes before serving.

Sriacha Chicken Wings

Prep time: 5 minutes
Cook time: 30 minutes
Serves: 2

Ingredients:
- 14-16 party chicken wings (with tips removed)
- 1/3 cup honey
- 2 Tbsp. sriracha sauce
- 4 tsp. soy sauce
- 1 Tbsp. butter
- 3 Tbsp. lime juice
- Salt and pepper to taste

Instructions:
1. Preheat air fryer to 360 degrees. Rinse wings and pat dry with a paper towel, then spray lightly with cooking spray. Sprinkle with salt and pepper. Air fry for a half hour, turning every 7-8 minutes.
2. In the meantime, combine lime juice, sriracha sauce, soy sauce, honey and butter in a small sauce pot. Cook over medium heat until it comes to a boil, stirring frequently. Boil for three minutes and remove from heat.
3. When the chicken wings are ready, remove from the air pot and add to a bowl. While still hot, toss with the sriracha sauce and serve.

Fried Chicken Wontons

The chicken flavor bursts through the crispy outer wonton shells.

Prep time: 15 minutes
Cook time: 12 minutes
Serves: 2

Ingredients:
- 1 package wonton wrappers
- 1 cup minced cooked chicken
- ¼ onion, chopped
- 1 egg
- ½ carrot, finely chopped
- ¼ tsp. soy sauce
- 2 tsp. coriander leaves, finely chopped
- ¼ tsp. chili powder
- ½ tsp. cornstarch
- ½ tsp. sesame oil

Instructions:
1. Preheat the air fryer to 350 degrees.
2. Combine chicken, egg, onions, carrots, chili powder coriander, soy sauce, corn starch and salt and pepper to taste. Add a drizzle of sesame seed oil and mix again.
3. Take chicken mixture, about 1 teaspoon at a time. Place in the center of a wonton wrapper. Wet the two edges of the wrapper, fold over in a crescent shape and seal. Repeat with remaining filling
4. Brush the prepared wontons with a little oil and add to the air fryer basket. Air fry for about 7 minutes, then turn and cook for another 3 minutes.

Chicken Parmesan with Sauce

Love chicken Parmesan? Wait until you try this low calorie, low fat version. Even with the cheese, you can eat it guilt free!

Prep time: 10 minutes
Cook time: 10 minutes
Serves: 2

Ingredients:

- 1 boneless skinless chicken breasts, sliced and half
- ½ cup panko bread crumbs
- ¼ cup Parmesan cheese
- ¼ cup mozzarella cheese
- 1 egg, beaten
- ½ cup marinara sauce
- Dash of Italian seasoning
- Dash of salt
- Dash of pepper

Instructions:

1. Heat fryer to 400 degrees. Spray basket with a small coating of cooking spray.
2. Slice the chicken breast horizontally. Place pieces between sheets of plastic wrap and pound until thin.
3. Combine bread crumbs with the Parmesan cheese and seasonings. Mix well and set aside.
4. In a separate bowl, dip the chicken pieces in the egg. Then dredge in the breadcrumb mixture.
5. Place the chicken pieces in the air fryer, and lightly coat the tops with cooking spray. Cook for about 7 minutes.
6. Next, top with sauce and then a layer of the mozzarella cheese.
7. Cook for 3 more minutes, or until the cheese has melted. Serve.

Chicken Croquettes

This recipe is a traditional option for Thanksgiving leftovers, but it's a great recipe to mix up either leftover chicken or turkey.

Prep time: 15 minutes
Cook time: 10 minutes
Serves: 2

Ingredients:
- ½ cup turkey or chicken, cooked, chopped
- 1 cup prepared stuffing
- 1 egg
- 3 Tbsp. cornstarch
- 2/3 cup turkey or chicken gravy
- ¼ cup cranberry sauce
- 1/2 cup panko bread crumbs

Instructions:
1. Preheat air fryer to 380 degrees.
2. Take about 2 tablespoons of the leftover turkey or chicken, roll into a ball and surround it with about 2 tablespoons of stuffing. Roll into balls. Repeat with remaining chicken and stuffing.
3. In a bowl, beat the egg. In another bowl, add the cornstarch and in a third bowl, all the panko bread crumbs.
4. Roll the chicken/turkey ball in the cornstarch, then dip into the egg mixture. Finally, dredge in the bread crumbs and set aside. Repeat the process with the remaining balls.
5. Grease your air fryer basket with oil and spritz additional oil on each croquette. Put as many croquettes in the basket without touching and cook for 6 minutes. Turn and cook for about 4 more minutes, or until fully browned on all sides.
6. Dip cooked croquettes in gravy and serve with cranberry sauce.

Chicken Tenders

The secret to these juicy chicken tenders is to marinade them in buttermilk for several hours before cooking. Between the buttermilk bath and the crispy crust, you'll want to keep this recipe front and center.

Prep time: 35 minutes
Cook time: 10 minutes
Serves: 2

Ingredients:

- ½ lb. chicken meat, cut into about 5-8 chicken tenders
- 2/3 cup buttermilk
- ¼ cup flour
- 1/8 tsp. baking powder
- 2/3 cup panko bread crumbs
- 2 Tbsp. butter, melted
- Dash of salt and pepper
- ¼ tsp. celery salt
- Dash oregano
- Dash cayenne pepper
- Dash thyme
- ½ tsp. paprika

Instructions:

1. Cut chicken into tender sized pieces. Place in a zippered storage bag with the buttermilk. Seal the bag and marinate for at least one half hour. Ideally, the chicken would marinade in the buttermilk for several hours.
2. When ready, preheat the air fryer to 350 degrees.
3. In a bowl, combine the flour, baking powder, spices and bread crumbs.
4. Take chicken strips from the marinade one at a time. Dredge in breadcrumb mixture, coating both sides.
5. Place prepared chicken strips in the air fryer and cook for 4 minutes. Brush chicken with melted butter, flip and cook for an additional 6 to 8 minutes until they are a crispy golden brown. The internal temperature should reach 175 degrees.

Seafood

Have you ever driven along a network of coastal towns and desperately wanted to stop as the seafood shacks alone the way tempted you with the succulent scents of fried foods? With the air fryer, you can bring the coast and all of its fried delights right to your dining room without the heavy feeling you get after binging on a traditional basket of fish and chips.

Give these recipes from under the sea a whirl, knowing you won't be breaking your diet (or the bank to fund a trip to the coast)!

Maryland Crab Cakes

This traditional crab cake recipe takes on a new twist with the air fryer. Serve with your favorite sauce, or just eat straight off the plate—you can't go wrong with these cakes.

Prep time: 10 minutes
Cook time: 22 minutes
Serves: 2

Ingredients:
- ¾ lb. crab meat
- ½ butter cracker crumbs, crumbled
- ½ tsp. celery seed
- 1 clove garlic, minced
- 2 Tbsp. parsley, chopped
- ¾ cup mayonnaise
- 1 tsp. sweet chili sauce
- 2 tsp. Thai chili sauce
- 1 tsp. Old Bay Seasoning
- 2 tsp. lemon juice
- Salt and pepper to taste

Instructions:
1. Preheat air fryer to 350 degrees.
2. Combine all ingredients, except for the cracker crumbs and crab meat. After thoroughly combined, gently fold in the crab and about ½ of the cracker crumbs.

3. Spread remaining crumbs on a cutting board or other work surface.
4. Form crab mixture into 8 evenly sized balls. Roll balls in the crumbs to evenly coat. Press the balls gently to form a patty and refrigerate for about 15 minutes.
5. Lightly spray crab cakes with cooking oil spray on both sides and add to preheated air fryer. Cook for about 10 minutes. Flip and cook for another 12 minutes. Serve warm.

Fried Fish and Chips

Don't forget to bring the malt vinegar to the table when serving up this hearty fare.

Prep time: 15 minutes
Cook time: 35 minutes
Serves: 2

Ingredients:
For the fries (chips):
- 1 large Russet potato, cut into strips about ½ inch thick
- 1 Tbsp. canola oil
- Salt

For the fish:
- 2 white fish filets, about 6 oz. each
- 3 Tbsp. flour
- 1 egg
- ½ Dijon mustard
- 2/3 cup Panko bread crumbs
- 1 tsp. olive oil

Instructions:
1. Cut the potato slices evenly and soak in a large bowl of salted water for about a half hour. Drain and pat dry with a paper towel.
2. Next, preheat the air fryer to 350 degrees.
3. While the fryer is preheating, put the fries in a large bowl with the canola oil and toss until it they are well coated. Air fry for about 20-25 minutes, stirring every 5 minutes or so to evenly cook the fries. When they are crisp, remove and sprinkle with salt. Set aside in a warm oven on a baking sheet.
4. Next, heat the fryer to 370 degrees.
5. Spread the flour on a clean cooking surface.
6. In a separate bowl, beat the egg and combine with the mustard. In another bowl, mix the bread crumbs with the olive oil.
7. Dredge the fish in flour and the dip in the egg bath. Finally dip in the crumb mixture. Place the fish in the fryer basket and cook in the air fryer for about 10 minutes, or until the fish shows doneness by flaking when tested with a fork.
8. Serve the fish with the warm fries and tartar sauce on the side.

Old Fashioned Fish Fry

Sometimes it's nice just to go back to a basic recipe and enjoy the simplicity that it entails, without all the extra taste profiles.

Prep time: 10 minutes
Cook time: 12 minutes
Serves: 2

Ingredients:
- 2 white fish filets
- 2/3 cup bread crumbs
- 1 egg
- 4 Tbsp, olive oil

Instructions:
1. Heat your air fryer to 350 degrees.
2. Combine the oil and breadcrumbs together, stirring until the bread crumbs are well saturated with the oil.
3. Whisk the egg in a separate bowl and remove any excess egg. Dip in the crumb mix making sure the fish is well coated.
4. Lay the filets in the air fryer, cooking for about 8 minutes. Flip and cook for an additional 4 minutes.
5. Serve immediately.

Air Fried Shrimp

The air fryer delicately brings out the sweetness of the shrimp in this low fat recipe.

Prep time: 10 minutes
Cook time: 20 minutes
Serves: 2

Ingredients:
- ½ lb. raw shrimp, peeled and deveined
- 1 egg, whisked
- 1/3 cup flour
- ¾ cup panko bread crumbs
- Old Bay Seasoning to taste
- Salt and Pepper to taste

For the sauce:
- 1/3 cup Greek yogurt, plain
- 3 Tbsp. sweet chili sauce
- 2 Tbsp. sriracha sauce

Instructions:
1. Heat air fryer to 400 degrees.
2. Sprinkle the shrimp with the Old Bay Seasoning and set aside. In one bowl, add the flour. In another bowl, whisk the egg and then add the panko bread crumbs.
3. Dredge the shrimp in the flour, then coat with the egg, followed by a dip in the panko bread crumbs.
4. Carefully spray the prepared shrimp with cooking spray. Cook the shrimp in the air fryer for 4 minutes. Flip over and cook for an extra 4 minutes.
5. In the meantime, prepare the sauce by combining the sriracha sauce, chili sauce and Greek yogurt. Mix thoroughly. Serve with cooked shrimp.

Air Fried Cod Sandwiches

There is something particularly comforting about a warm, crispy fish filet in a delicious bun for lunch or a light dinner.

Prep time: 5 minutes
Cook time: 10 minutes
Serves: 2

Ingredients:
- 2 cod filets, about 4 oz. each
- 1 egg
- 2 Tbsp. Panko bread crumbs
- 2 bulkie rolls
- 2 leaves of lettuce
- Tartar sauce

Instructions:
1. Heat air fryer to 400 degrees.
2. Pat fish dry. In one bowl, beat the egg and in a second bowl, toss the Panko break crumbs with a dash of salt.
3. Dip the fish in the egg and then dredge it in the bread crumbs on both sides.
4. Carefully spray each side with oil. Place in the fryer and cook for about 5 minutes. Carefully flip and cook for an additional 5 minutes.
5. Build your fish burger by placing the slightly cooled fish in a bun and topping with tartar sauce and lettuce.

Tuna Cakes

Tuna cakes are so deliciously crunchy with the celery, and now they are even healthier when cooked in the air fryer.

Prep time: 6 minutes
Cook time: 11 minutes
Serves: 2

Ingredients:

- 1 can of tuna
- 1 egg
- 3 Tbsp. mayonnaise
- 1/3 cup bread crumbs
- 1/3 cup minced onion
- 1 stalk of celery, minced
- ½ bell pepper, minced
- 2 Tbsp. chili sauce
- ½ tsp. Worcestershire sauce

Instructions:

1. Heat air fryer to 380 degrees
2. Drain water from the can of tuna and put the tuna in a small mixing bowl. Combine remaining ingredients with the tuna. Form into 2 patties.
3. Spray the bottom of the fryer basket with cooking oil. Carefully lay the tuna patties in the fryer basket and then lightly spritz the tops of the patties with a little more oil.
4. Air fry for 6 minutes, then carefully flip the patties over and cook for another 5 minutes.
5. Serve on a bun or with tartar sauce.

Cajun Shrimp Fry

Bring the flavors and scents of New Orleans and Cajun Country into your kitchen with this delicious, low fat recipe!

Prep time: 8 minutes
Cook time: 8 minutes
Serves: 2

Ingredients:
- ¾ lb. shrimp, peeled and deveined
- ¾ tsp. Old Bay Seasoning
- ¼ tsp. cayenne pepper
- Pam or other cooking spray
- 2/3 cup ketchup
- 2/3 cup chili sauce
- 1 Tbsp. grated horseradish
- ¾ tsp. Worcestershire sauce
- Juice of one half lemon

Instructions:
1. Preheat the air fryer to 390 degrees.
2. In a bowl, combine the cayenne pepper and Old Bay Seasoning. Toss the mixture with the shrimp, coating it evenly.
3. Lightly spray the bottom of the air fryer basket with cooking spray. Place the shrimp in the basket and spritz the top of the shrimp with a little cooking spray. Cook for 6 to 8 minutes, depending on the size of the shrimp. Give the basket a good shake about halfway through the cooking time.
4. In the meantime, prepare the cocktail sauce by combining the ketchup, chili sauce, Worcestershire sauce, lemon juice and horseradish. Serve on the side as a dipping sauce for the Cajun shrimp.

Air Fried Salmon

Just when you didn't think salmon couldn't get any healthier, here comes an additional way to cut fat in the air fryer.

Prep time: 5 minutes
Cook time: 10 minutes
Serves: 2

Ingredients:
- 2 salmon filets, about 5 oz. each
- 2 tsp. olive oil
- 1 tsp. paprika
- Dash of Old Bay Seasoning
- Salt and pepper to taste

Instructions:
1. Check salmon for any rogue bones and remove them. Let sit while the air fryer is preheating to 390 degrees.
2. When the air fryer is heated, rub the salmon with oil, then sprinkle with salt, pepper and Old Bay Seasoning.
3. Place filets in the air fryer basket. Cook for about 7 minutes, then check for doneness. If not flaking, cook for an additional minute or two until cooked to taste.
4. Serve with lemon wedges.

Fish Tacos

These tacos are a great way to add fish to your diet, and they are so easy to assemble and eat.

Prep time: 10 minutes
Cook time: 12 minutes
Serves: 2

Ingredients:
- ½ lb. tilapia filets
- 2 flour tortillas
- ½ cup flour
- ½ cup ice water
- 1 tsp. yellow mustard
- 2/3 cup panko bread crumbs
- ½ coleslaw mix
- 2 Tbsp. mayonnaise

Instructions:
1. Heat the air fryer to 370 degrees.
2. Cut the filets into bite sized pieces.
3. In a bowl, combine the flour, ice water and yellow mustard, whisking well. In another bowl, add the bread crumbs.
4. Dredge the fish pieces in the flour mixture, letting the excess batter drip off. Next, coat the battered fish in bread crumbs, pressing the crumbs into the batter.
5. Lightly grease the fryer basket and add the fish pieces. Spray the tops with a little more cooking oil.
6. Cook for 6 minutes. Then, shake the fryer basket and flip the fish pieces over and cook for an additional 6 minutes.
7. Remove from fryer and allow to cool for 2 to 3 minutes.
8. Lay the fish in the center of the tortillas, lightly spread the mayonnaise and top with the coleslaw mix.
9. Serve immediately.

Blackened Shrimp

If you like a lot of extra kick, serve with a spicy dipping sauce, or balance out the spices with a cooler tarter sauce.

Prep time: 5 minutes
Cook time: 7 minutes
Serves: 2

Ingredients:
- 1 ½ lb. jumbo shrimp, deveined and peeled
- Cooking spray
- 2 tsp. paprika
- 2 tsp. garlic salt
- 1 ½ tsp. onion powder
- 1 tsp. dried cumin
- ¾ tsp. oregano
- ¼ tsp. cayenne pepper
- ½ tsp. red pepper flakes
- Salt and pepper to taste

Instructions:
1. Preheat the air fryer to 390 degrees.
2. In a bag, combine the paprika, salt and pepper, cumin, oregano, cayenne pepper, red pepper flakes, garlic salt and onion powder. Mix well.
3. Lightly spray both sides of the shrimp with the cooking spray. Add the shrimp to the bag and toss well, evenly coating the shrimp with the spices. Cook for 7 minutes. Give the basket a good shake about halfway through the cooking time.

Air Fried Tilapia

The air fryer does an amazing job in bringing out the flavors of this delicate fish.

Prep time: 2 minutes
Cook time: 7 minutes
Serves: 2

Ingredients:
- 1 lb. tilapia filets
- ½ tsp. Old Bay Seasoning
- ¼ tsp. lemon pepper
- Olive oil

Instructions:
1. Heat air fryer to 400 degrees. When up to temperature, spray the basket with olive oil or another cooking spray.
2. Place tilapia filets in the basket, spray lightly with oil and add spices.
3. Cook for about 7 minutes, depending on the thickness of the fish. When it flakes with a fork, remove and serve.

Fish Nuggets

Prep time: 8 minutes
Cook time: 12 minutes
Serves: 2

Ingredients:
- 2 cup haddock or other whitefish
- ½ cup Panko bread crumbs
- ½ tsp. Old Bay Seasoning
- 3 Tbsp. flour
- 1 egg
- ½ cup tartar sauce

Instructions:
1. Heat the air fryer to 400 degrees.
2. Rinse fish and pat dry with a paper towel. Cut into equal pieces, about 1 1/2 inches square. (You don't need to be exact with this, but it gives an idea of the size pieces.)
3. In a bowl, beat the egg and mix in about 1 Tbsp. water. In a separate bowl, add the flour and Old Bay Seasoning, stir well. Slowly drizzle in the egg mixture, whipping the mixture with a whisk to remove the lumps. If necessary, add a little more water until the batter is the consistency of pancake batter.
4. Put the bread crumbs in a separate bowl.
5. Take the fish pieces and dredge in the batter. Allow the excess batter to run off and then put the battered fish in the bread crumbs. You can press lightly to ensure an even coating of crumbs.
6. Lightly spray the cooking basket of the air fryer. Lay the pieces of fish in the basket, making sure not to overcrowd the basket. If you have a smaller air fryer, you might need to cook this in two batches.
7. Fry for about 6 minutes, then give the basket a good shake and cook for an additional 4 to 6 minutes, depending on the thickness of the fish.
8. Serve warm with tartar sauce on the side.

Air Fried Scallops

Make sure you use large bay scallops for this recipe; otherwise, the small ones may overcook and become rubbery.

Prep time: 2 minutes
Cook time: 4 minutes
Serves: 2

Ingredients:
- 1 lb. scallops
- 2 Tbsp. butter
- Salt and Pepper to taste

Instructions:
1. Heat air fryer to 390 degrees.
2. Rinse scallops and pat dry with a paper towel.
3. Melt butter and toss scallops in the melted butter. Sprinkle with salt and pepper.
4. Add scallops to the air fryer basket and cook for 2 minutes. Flip over and cook for an additional 2 minutes.

Shrimp Scampi

Using the air fryer to cook the shrimp gives it a delightful, sweet taste—a perfect complement to the other flavors in your recipe.

Prep time: 5 minutes
Cook time: 10 minutes
Serves: 2

Ingredients:
- ½ lb. shrimp, peeled and deveined
- 3 Tbsp. butter
- 1 Tbsp. minced garlic
- ½ tsp. lemon juice
- 1 Tbsp. white wine
- 1 tsp. red pepper flakes
- Prepared pasta or zoodles (optional)

Instructions:
1. If desired, cook your favorite pasta.
2. Preheat air fryer to 330 degrees. Carefully place a small metal pan on the frying rack.
3. Add garlic, butter and red pepper flakes to the pan. Cook for about 2 minutes, stirring to ensure butter doesn't burn.
4. Add the chicken stock or white wine, then the shrimp, stirring gently to coat the shrimp.
5. Air fry for 5 minutes, stirring halfway through cooking. If desired, sprinkle with basil leaves and serve with pasta or zoodles.

Vegan & Vegetarian

Air fried foods aren't just meat and potatoes. There are so many vegan and vegetarian recipes that you can use for a lower cholesterol option.

With the air fryer and a little spritz of oil, you can spice up your vegetarian options with these deliciously crispy recipes.

Roasted Corn

Believe it or not, corn in the air fryer is a delicious way to serve up this popular summer vegetable.

Prep time: 10 minutes
Cook time: 10 minutes
Serves: 2

Ingredients:
- 2 ears of corn
- 2 tsp. melted butter or olive oil
- Salt and pepper

Instructions:
1. Preheat air fryer to 400 degrees
2. Prepare your corn by removing the husks and washing. If necessary, trim the ends of the corn so they'll fit in the air fryer basket. Remember you don't want to overcrowd the basket.
3. Place the corn in the air fryer and drizzle with melted butter or oil, then sprinkle with salt and pepper.
4. Cook for about 10 minutes.

Stuffed Banana Peppers

Also known as Bharwaan Mirchi, this dish is adapted from the traditional Indian fare. Cook them up without the guilt of the extra oil.

Prep time: 10 minutes
Cook time: 8 minutes
Serves: 2

Ingredients:
- 10 banana peppers
- 1 ½ cup mashed potatoes
- ½ cup onion, chopped
- 2 Tbsp. coriander
- ½ tsp. turmeric
- ½ tsp. red chili powder
- 1 Tbsp. lemon juice
- Salt and pepper to taste

Instructions:
1. Combine the prepared mashed potatoes with the onion, spices and lemon juice.
2. Cut the peppers in half lengthwise and remove seeds. Lightly spray oil on all sides of the peppers, then fill pepper halves with the potato mixture.
3. Place aluminum foil on the Air fryer's wire rack. Preheat to 350 degrees.
4. Lay the peppers in the wire rack and fry for 6 to 8 minutes.

Air Fried Pita Pizza

This makes a delicious lunch or quick dinner on a busy day. Or cook some up while watching your favorite movie—the first one will be done practically before the opening credits are finished.

Prep time: 4 minutes
Cook time: 6 minutes
Serves: 2

Ingredients:
- 2 pita bread rounds
- 2 Tbsp. pizza sauce
- 1 1/3 cup mozzarella cheese
- Olive oil
- Desired toppings

Instructions:
1. Preheat air fryer to 350 degrees.
2. Using a spoon, evenly spread pizza sauce on the pita bread. Top with cheese and desired toppings. Finally, drizzle top of pizza with about 1 tsp. of olive oil.
3. Place pizza carefully in the air fryer. Cover with an inverted trivet, if available. Fry for 6 minutes.
4. Carefully remove trivet and then the pizza from the oven. Set aside and repeat with second pita pizza.
5. Cut into slices and serve.

Cauliflower Rice

In the trend to eat healthier, cauliflower rice is emerging as a delicious, low calorie alternative to traditional rice.

Prep time: 5 minutes
Cook time: 10 minutes
Serves: 2

Ingredients:
- ½ head cauliflower
- ½ cup chopped broccoli
- 2/3 cup frozen peas
- 2 Tbsp. soy sauce
- 1 tsp. sesame oil
- 2 tsp. rice vinegar
- ½ tsp. minced ginger
- ½ cup chopped broccoli

Instructions:
1. Prepare the cauliflower by steaming for about 5-8 minutes, then pulsing in the food processor until they resemble rice. You can skip this step by purchasing frozen riced cauliflower.
2. Preheat air fryer to 370 degrees.
3. Toss the riced cauliflower with the remaining ingredients, mixing well. Place in a metal dish in the air fryer and cook for about 5 minutes. Stir gently and cook for another 5 minutes.

Kale Chips

Kale chips are a delicious snack or appetizer, but to maintain the crispiness, they should be eaten immediately after cooking.

Prep time: 5 minutes
Cook time: 5 minutes
Serves: 2

Ingredients:
- 4 cup kale, stems removed
- 3 Tbsp. coconut oil
- Salt and pepper to taste

Instructions:
1. Heat air fryer to 370 degrees.
2. Rub the coconut oil on the kale pieces, then toss with salt and pepper.
3. Add the kale to your air fryer and cook for about 2 minutes. Stir and cook for an additional 2 to 3 minutes. Serve immediately.

Tofu Scramble

While the tofu scramble has a lot of different steps, the end result is a delicious, well-balanced meal sure to please.

Prep time: 5 minutes
Cook time: 30 minutes
Serves: 2

Ingredients:
- ½ block of tofu
- 1 Tbsp. soy sauce
- 1 tsp. olive oil
- 1 cup red potato, cubed
- 1/3 cup chopped onion
- 2 cup broccoli florets
- ¼ tsp. garlic powder
- ½ tsp. turmeric

Instructions:
1. Heat air fryer to 400 degrees.
2. In a bowl, combine tofu, a dash of olive oil, soy sauce, garlic powder, onion powder, onion and turmeric. Set aside and allow the tofu to marinate in the flavors.
3. Next, in another bowl, toss the potatoes with the olive oil and a dash of salt. Add the potatoes to the air fryer and cook for about 7 minutes. Stir and cook for another 7 to 8 minutes.
4. Stir the potatoes a second time and add the tofu. Don't discard any leftover marinate but set it aside for later.
5. Cook the tofu and potato mixture for about 10 minutes.
6. In the meantime, combine the broccoli florets with the tofu marinade, adding a dash of soy sauce if necessary to coat all the broccoli.
7. Add to the potatoes and tofu in the air fryer and cook for another 5 minutes.
8. Serve immediately.

Jalapeno Peppers

The air fryer does a fantastic job of crisping up the skin of the jalapeno, a delightful contrast to the cream cheese insides.

Prep time: 5 minutes
Cook time: 8 minutes
Serves: 2

Ingredients:
- 10 jalapenos
- 1 cup cream cheese
- 2/3 cup bread crumbs
- 3 Tbsp. fresh parsley

Instructions:
1. Heat the air fryer to 370 degrees.
2. Slice the jalapenos in half lengthwise and remove the stems and seeds.
3. Combine about one third cup of bread crumbs with the cream cheese and stuff each pepper. Coat with the remaining bread crumbs, gently pressing the crumbs into the cream cheese mixture so they don't fall off.
4. Cook for about 6 to 8 minutes.
5. Cool slightly and serve.

Air Fried Ravioli

This meal is easy to prepare and ready in no time!

Prep time: 5 minutes
Cook time: 5 minutes
Serves: 2

Ingredients:
- 1 package of cheese or squash ravioli
- 2/3 cup buttermilk
- 1 jar marinara sauce
- 1 Tbsp. olive oil
- 1/3 C grated Parmesan cheese
- 1 ½ cup bread crumbs

Instructions:
1. Heat air fryer to 200 degrees.
2. Combine bread crumbs with the olive oil and set aside.
3. Dip ravioli in buttermilk then press the breadcrumb mixture onto the tops.
4. Cover frying rack with parchment paper and place the ravioli on the parchment. Air fry for about 5 minutes.
5. In the meantime, heat the marinara sauce.
6. When ready, serve the fried ravioli with marinara sauce, topped with grated Parmesan.

Sweet Potato Fries

Love sweet potato fries? You're going to enjoy them even more when they come out of the air fryer with a perfect, crispy outside!

Prep time: 5 minutes
Cook time: 16 minutes
Serves: 2

Ingredients:
- 1 large sweet potato
- ¼ cup olive oil
- 1 tsp. dried mustard
- Salt and pepper to taste

Instructions:
1. Heat air fryer to 350 degrees.
2. Peel the sweet potato and cut them into long fry shapes. Coat with olive oil until the fries are coated evenly with oil. Sprinkle with a dash of salt.
3. Cook for about 8 minutes, then give the frying basket a shake to mix up the sweet potato fries. Cook for another 8 minutes or until done.
4. Remove from the air fryer. Toss with additional olive oil, dried mustard and salt and pepper. Serve.

Fried Brussels Sprouts

Air frying these delicious vegetables brings out the sweet taste. It's a perfect complement to the vinegar and salt.

Prep time: 3 minutes
Cook time: 8-10 minutes
Serves: 2

Ingredients:
- 1 cup fresh Brussels sprouts
- 1 Tbsp. olive oil
- 1 Tbsp. balsamic vinegar
- Salt and pepper to taste

Instructions:
1. Heat the air fryer to 400 degrees.
2. Cut the Brussels sprouts in half lengthwise. Toss with the olive oil, vinegar, salt and pepper.
3. Add to the air fryer and cook for about 5 minutes. Shake the basket and cook for another 3 to 5 minutes, watching carefully during the last few minutes to make sure the vegetable doesn't burn.

Grilled Tomatoes

There is something about grilled or fried tomatoes that brings summertime directly into your kitchen, no matter what time of the year it is!

Prep time: 3 minutes
Cook time: 18 minutes
Serves: 2

Ingredients:
- 2 large vine-ripened tomatoes
- ½ tsp. parsley
- ¼ tsp. rosemary
- 1 tsp. olive oil
- Salt and pepper to taste

Instructions:
1. Preheat air fryer to 320 degrees.
2. Wash the tomatoes and cut in half. Spritz with olive oil. Sprinkle with sale and pepper, rosemary and parsley. You can also substitute your favorite herbs, such as basil, thyme, oregano or sage.
3. Place tomato slices in the fryer, cut side up.
4. Cook for about 15 minutes. Check for doneness and cook for an additional 3 to 5 minutes, if necessary.

Air Fried Baked Potatoes

The cooking time is going to vary greatly, depending on the size of your potatoes.

Prep time: 5 minutes
Cook time: 18-20 minutes
Serves: 2

Ingredients:
- 2 Russet potatoes
- 2 tsp. butter
- ¼ cup sour cream
- ¼ cup grated cheddar cheese
- 1 tsp. chives
- Salt and pepper to taste

Instructions:
1. Preheat air fryer to 350 degrees. Pierce the skin of the potatoes with a fork.
2. Place potatoes in the air fryer and cook for about 15 minutes.
3. In the meantime, combine the sour cream, chives and cheese. Set aside.
4. Check potatoes and cook for an additional 5 minutes, or until the insides are soft.
5. When ready, cut the potatoes open. Spread with butter, and top with the sour cream mixture.

Air Fried Rice Balls

Also known as Arancini, this traditional Italian dish is often served during festivals or holidays. While these are great for a buffet item, they are also delicious as a main dish for two people.

Prep time: 8 minutes
Cook time: 10 minutes
Serves: 2

Ingredients:

- 1 cup arborino rice, cooked
- 3 Tbsp. parsley
- 3 Tbsp. Parmesan cheese
- 2 eggs
- 1 cup seasoned bread crumbs
- ½ cup panko break crumbs
- Olive oil
- 1 jar prepared marinara sauce

Instructions:

1. The day before making this recipe, cook the rice and allow it to rest for a day.
2. Preheat air fryer to 340 degrees
3. Separate one egg and beat the egg white. Discard the yolk. Set the egg white aside.
4. Combine bread crumbs in another bowl and set aside.
5. Combine chilled rice with the egg, cheese, parsley, salt and pepper. Mix well with your hands.
6. Form rice into balls, roll in beaten egg white and then in the bread crumbs.
7. Spray the basket with a little cooking oil. Place rice balls in the air frying basket and spritz them with additional cooking oil. Cook for about 5 minutes. Give the basket a little shake and cook for another 3 to 5 minutes or until the rice balls are a nice golden brown.
8. Serve with marinara sauce.

Chinese Orange Tofu

Try this favorite Chinese dish without the fat, gluten, or guilt!

Prep time: 15 minutes
Cook time: 20 minutes
Serves: 2

Ingredients:
- ½ lb. tofu, extra firm
- 2 tsp. tamari
- 2 tsp. cornstarch, separated
- ½ tsp. orange zest
- ¼ cup orange juice
- ½ cup water
- Dash of red pepper flakes
- 1 tsp. maple syrup
- ½ tsp. minced garlic
- ½ tsp. fresh minced ginger

Instructions:
1. Heat air fryer to 390 degrees.
2. Cut tofu into cubes and put in a large plastic storage bag with the tamari, shaking gently until the tofu is coated completely.
3. Add 1 teaspoon of cornstarch to the bag and shake again. Set aside so the tofu can absorb the flavors for about 15 minutes.
4. In the meantime, combine the remaining ingredients in a small bowl. Stir thoroughly and set aside.
5. Add tofu to the air fryer, making sure to put the tofu in a single layer, and not stacking on top if itself.
6. Cook for 5 minutes. Give the basket a shake and cook for another 5d minutes.
7. When the tofu is cooked, add it to a frying pan over medium high heat. Pour the orange sauce over the tofu and cook until the sauce has thickened.
8. Serve alone or with rice.

Fried Falafel

Falafel is incredibly versatile. These fried balls can be eaten alone, used to top salads or enjoyed in a pita pocket.

Prep time: 30 minutes
Cook time: 12 minutes
Serves: 2

Ingredients:
- 1 can of chickpeas, drained and rinsed
- 1 cup rolled oats
- 1/3 cup onion, diced
- 2/3 carrots, minced
- ½ cup roasted cashews
- 2 Tbsp. soy sauce
- 1 Tbsp. flax meal
- ¼ cup lemon juice
- ¾ tsp. ground cumin
- ½ tsp. turmeric
- 1 tsp. garlic powder

Instructions:
1. Heat air fryer to 370 degrees.
2. In a frying pan, heat the olive oil. Cook onions and carrots for about 5 minutes. Set aside.
3. Blend the cashews and oats in the food processor and add to the onion mixture.
4. Next, add the chickpeas in the food processor, adding the soy sauce and lemon juice. Puree. Add to the onion mixture and stir in spices and flax meal, combining thoroughly.
5. Roll mixture into 12 even balls and arrange in the air fryer basket.
6. Cook for about 8 minutes. Give the basket a shake and cook for another 4 minutes.
7. Serve immediately or reserve for later falafel use.

Jicama Fries

If you haven't had a chance to try a jicama yet, you're missing out. Although it looks like a rutabaga, don't be fooled. The jicama texture will remind you of an apple, with a light, sweet combination of an apple and a pear.

Prep time: 5 minutes
Cook time: 20 minutes
Serves: 2

Ingredients:
- ½ jicama
- 2 eggs, beaten
- 2/3 cup arrowroot flour
- ½ tsp. salt

Instructions:
1. Heat the air fryer to 390 degrees.
2. Peel the half of a jicama and cut into fry shapes. In a bowl, carefully combine the jicama slices with the beaten egg.
3. In another bowl, combine the salt and arrowroot flour. Toss the fries in the flour mixture, a few at a time and set aside the coated fries until they are all coated.
4. Lightly spray the bottom of the cooking basket with oil and add the jicama fries.
5. Cook for 10 minutes, then give the basket a good toss to mix up the fries. Cook for 10 more minutes.
6. Serve immediately.

Fried Artichoke Hearts

Pair these with an aioli, use as a pasta topping or just eat them right out of the fryer. These fried artichoke hearts are amazingly versatile.

Prep time: 8 minutes
Cook time: 8 minutes
Serves: 2

Ingredients:

- 14 canned artichoke hearts, liquid removed
- 2/3 cup flour
- 7 Tbsp. panko bread crumbs
- ¼ tsp. baking powder
- 6-7 Tbsp. water
- Dash of dried basil
- Dash of oregano
- Dash of smoked paprika
- Dash of garlic powder
- Canola oil for spraying

Instructions:

1. Heat the air fryer to 360 degrees.
2. Drain artichoke hearts. Place on paper towels and press leaves lightly to absorb additional liquid.
3. In a bowl, combine flour, baking powder, water and a little salt and pepper, to taste. If needed, add a little more water, so the batter resembles pancake batter in consistency.
4. In another bowl, combine the bread crumbs with the seasonings.
5. Dip the artichoke hearts in the batter, fully coating the vegetable. Remove excess batter and roll in the bread crumbs until fully coated.
6. Place all the battered artichoke hearts in the fryer basket and spritz with a little oil if desired.
7. Cook for about 4 minutes. Flip and cook for an additional 4 minutes.

Avocado Fries

If possible, avoid using overripe avocados in this recipe, because a firmer avocado will hold up much better under cooking.

Prep time: 10 minutes
Cook time: 10 minutes
Serves: 2

Ingredients:
- 2 avocados, ripe but not overripe
- ½ cup panko bread crumbs
- ½ cup bread crumbs
- Liquid from 2 cans of white or pinto beans
- Salt and pepper to taste

Instructions:
1. Combine panko bread crumbs and regular bread crumbs in a bowl with salt and pepper. In a separate bowl, pour the bean liquid (also called aquafaba).
2. Cut the avocados into wedges, probably 8-10 slices per avocado.
3. Dip the slices in the bean liquid and then coat with the bread crumb mixture.
4. Arrange in the air fryer basket. You'll probably need to do these in two batches, so they don't crowd in the fryer.
5. Turn the air fryer to 390 degrees and cook the slices for 5 minutes. Shake the basket and cook for another 5 minutes.
6. Serve in sandwiches or with an aioli sauce.

Pasta Chips

This recipe is great with bow-tie pasta, but could be used with any flat type of pasta. For a gluten-free experience, try a brown rice or bean pasta.

Prep time: 10 minutes
Cook time: 10 minutes
Serves: 2

Ingredients:
- 2 cup pasta
- 1 Tbsp. Olive Oil
- 2 tsp. Italian seasoning
- Salt and pepper to taste

Instructions
1. Preheat the air fryer to 390 degrees.
2. Partially cook the pasta, boiling it for about half of the package instructions. Drain.
3. Toss the pasta with remaining ingredients.
4. Place the pasta in the air fryer in a single layer. Depending on the size of your air fryer, you may need to cook these in two batches.
5. Cook for about 5 minutes. Give the basket a good shake and then fry for another 3 to 5 minutes. The pasta will be crunchy but will become even crispier when they are fully cool.

Fried Tortilla Chips

These tortilla chips are delicious alone or with salsa and are a much healthier alternative to prepackaged, processed chips.

Prep time: 3 minutes
Cook time: 8 minutes
Serves: 2

Ingredients:
- 2 tortillas
- 2 tsp. olive oil
- Sea salt

Instructions:
1. Heat your air fryer to 350 degrees.
2. Slice tortillas into quarters or eighths.
3. Coat both sides of the tortilla slices with olive oil and sprinkle with salt.
4. Air fry for about 4 minutes. Shake the basket and then fry for an additional 4 minutes.

Breakfast

Chances are, when you bought your air fryer, you were thinking about low fat alternatives to the traditional greasy, guilt-laden meals, like fish and chips, or chicken tenders. But did you ever think that there would be so many options for breakfast foods too?

And not just donuts (although those are a favorite breakfast staple). The air fryer is incredibly versatile, and you can enjoy everything from a delicious egg frittata to muffins. Even bagels can easily be made right in your kitchen, without the multitude of steps it usually takes to make a traditional bagel.

Hard Boiled Eggs

What? 'Hard boil' eggs in an air fryer? Absolutely!

Prep time: 1 minute
Cook time: 16 minutes
Serves: 2

Ingredients:
- 4 eggs

Instructions:
1. Keep the eggs in the refrigerator until you are ready to cook them.
2. Preheat the air fryer to 250 degrees and add the eggs to the wire rack. Cook for 15-17 minutes, depending on your fryer's wattage. When cooking time is complete, remove the eggs and immediately put them in a bowl of ice water to stop the cooking process.

French Toast Bites

Prep time: 5 minutes
Cook time: 15 minutes
Serves: 2

Ingredients:
- 4 slices bread
- 2 eggs
- 3 Tbsp. milk
- 2 Tbsp. sugar
- ½ tsp. cinnamon

Instructions:
1. Preheat the air fryer to 360 degrees.
2. Combine the eggs and milk. Cut the pieces of bread in half and rolls the halves into tight balls.
3. Dredge the bread balls in the egg mixture, letting the mixture soak into the bread a little bit.
4. In a separate bowl, combine the cinnamon and sugar. Roll the egg-soaked bread balls into the cinnamon and sugar. Make sure the balls are fully coated with cinnamon and sugar.
5. Add the bread balls to the air fryer and fry for 10 minutes. Give the basket a shake and fry for an additional 5 minutes.
6. Delicious alone or dunked in maple syrup.

Home Fried Potatoes

These have the deliciousness of home fries you'd get in your favorite greasy diner, but now you an enjoy them without all the fat!

Prep time: 30 minutes
Cook time: 35 minutes
Serves: 2

Ingredients:
- 3 potatoes, peeled and diced into ½ inch cubes
- 1 onion, diced
- ½ cup diced red pepper
- 2 Tbsp. ghee
- 1 tsp. garlic salt
- 1 tsp. onion powder
- 1 tsp. smoked paprika
- Salt and pepper to taste

Instructions:
1. Soak the diced potatoes in a large bowl of water for about 20 to 25 minutes.
2. In the meantime, combine the seasonings and set aside.
3. Heat the air fryer to 370 degrees. Drain the potatoes from the water and combine with the ghee. Add to the air fryer and cook for about 20 minutes, giving the basket a good shake every 5 minutes to allow it to mix well.
4. While the potatoes are cooking, put the diced onions and red peppers in the same bowl used to toss the potatoes and ghee.
5. After the potatoes have cooked for 20 minutes, remove the potatoes. Toss the potatoes with the onions and peppers, then toss in the seasoning. Add everything to the fryer basket.
6. Raise the temperature to 380 degrees and cook for about 5 minutes. Shake the basket and then cook for a final three minutes.

Cinnamon Rolls

These ooey-gooey rolls require a little patience, but they are so worth the wait when you start to smell them in the air fryer.

Prep time: 15 minutes
Rest time: 1 ½ to 2 hours
Cook time: 10 minutes
Serves: 2

Ingredients:
- ½ can bread dough, or ¼ lb. frozen bread dough, thawed
- 1 Tbsp. butter
- 1/3 cup brown sugar
- Dash of cinnamon
- 2 oz. cream cheese, room temperature
- 2 tsp. butter, room temperature
- 2/3 cup powdered sugar
- 1/8 tsp. vanilla

Instructions:
1. Roll the dough out on a floured surface to the size of a regular piece of paper, positioned horizontally so the long side is facing you.
2. Brush the melted tablespoon of butter over the dough. Combine the cinnamon with the brown sugar and sprinkle over the dough evenly.
3. Roll the dough tightly, pressing the edges together to ensure a tight seal.
4. Cut the dough log into 4 even rolls. Set aside to let rise for about 2 hours.
5. After the rolls have risen, heat the air fryer to 350 degrees. Add the rolls and fry for five minutes. Then turn them over and fry for an additional 4 to 5 minutes.
6. Remove from the air fryer and allow to cool for a few minutes. In the meantime, combine the remaining ingredients to make the glaze.
7. Glaze the cinnamon rolls while they are still warm and serve.

Breakfast Frittata

Frittatas are a delicious way to start your morning with the perfect balance of protein, cheese and vegetables.

Prep time: 10 minutes
Cook time: 10 minutes
Serves: 2

Ingredients:
- 3 eggs
- 1 Tbsp. milk
- ¼ cup cheddar cheese, or cheese of your choice
- 1/3 lb. sweet Italian sausage
- 4 cherry tomatoes, halved
- ¼ green pepper, diced
- Salt and pepper to taste

Instructions:
1. Preheat the air fryer to 360 degrees.
2. Fry the sausage on the stovetop. Drain and spread an even layer on the bottom of your fryer's baking accessory, if you have one. If not, you can use a metal dish that will fit in the air fryer.
3. Combine the eggs, milk, tomatoes, green pepper, salt and pepper. Pour mixture over the sausage. Air fry for 5 minutes.

Blueberry Muffins

Muffins in the air fryer cook faster than traditional baking and come out so delicious.

Prep time: 10 minutes
Cook time: 14 minutes
Serves: 2

Ingredients:
- ½ cup flour
- ¾ tsp. baking powder
- 3 Tbsp. sugar
- 3 Tbsp. canola oil
- 1/8 cup applesauce
- 3 Tbsp. sour cream
- 1/3 cup blueberries

Instructions:
1. Heat air fryer to 320 degrees.
2. Combine the flour, sugar and baking powder in a small bowl. Set aside.
3. In a medium sized bowl, combine the applesauce, sour cream, oil and applesauce. Blend well. Add the dry ingredients and stir by hand, until the dough is combined, being careful not to over-mix or it changes the final consistency of the muffins. Fold in the blueberries.
4. Spray 4 silicone muffin cups with oil. Evenly distribute the batter.
5. Put the cups in the air fryer and bake for 14 minutes.

Bran and Apple Muffins

This recipe is perfect with a bran bud cereal such as All Bran.

Prep time: 10 minutes
Cook time: 14 minutes
Serves: 2

Ingredients:
- ½ cup flour
- ½ tsp. baking powder
- 1 tsp. baking soda
- ½ cup bran cereal buds
- 2/3 cup apple, peeled and diced
- 2 Tbsp. brown sugar
- 2 Tbsp. oil
- 1 tsp. vanilla
- 1 egg
- 1/3 cup almond milk
- ½ tsp. cinnamon
- Dash of nutmeg

Instructions:
1. In a small bowl, combine the flour, baking powder, baking soda, cinnamon and nutmeg. Set aside.
2. In a medium sized bowl, whisk together the milk, egg, oil, vanilla and brown sugar Add the dry ingredients and stir by hand, until the dough is moist but not overworked.
3. Fold in apples and bran cereal.
4. Spray 4 silicone muffin cups with oil. Evenly distribute the batter.
5. Put the cups in the air fryer and bake for 14 minutes.

Breakfast Pockets

If serving to kids, remember that the filling may be very hot, even when the outside is cool enough to pick up.

Prep time: 15 minutes
Cook time: 7-10 minutes
Serves: 2

Ingredients:

- ½ box of puff pastry sheets
- 3 eggs
- 1 egg, whisked
- ¼ cup shredded cheddar cheese
- ¼ cup sweet Italian sausage, cooked and drained
- 4 strips of bacon, cooked and crumbled

Instructions:

1. Scramble the eggs and cook in a frying pan on the stove. Remove from heat and set aside.
2. Preheat air fryer to 370 degrees.
3. Lay out puff pastry sheets and cut out four rectangles, about 2 inches by 3 inches.
4. Layer egg, cooked bacon, cooked sausage and cheese on two of the squares, leaving a good edge around the sides.
5. Put the other pastry rectangles on the top of the first ones, and use a fork to seal the edges. If desired, brush the tops with the whisked egg or spray with cooking oil for a nice shine.
6. Place in the air fryer and cook for about 7 minutes. Check for doneness. If not brown and crispy, fry for another 2 to 3 minutes, checking every minute to prevent burning.
7. Allow to cool slightly and serve.

Monkey Bread

For an even lower fat option with this recipe, you can skip the butter and brown sugar. Simply spritz the top of the biscuit balls with cooking spray and add a few pinches of cinnamon sugar.

Prep time: 10 minutes
Cook time: 7 minutes
Serves: 2

Ingredients:
- 1 canister of refrigerated biscuits
- 2/3 cup sugar
- 2 tsp. cinnamon
- 4 Tbsp. butter
- 2/3 cup brown sugar

Instructions:
1. Heat the air fryer to 375 degrees.
2. Cut the biscuits into bite sized pieces and roll the gently into balls. Combine the sugar and cinnamon and put in a plastic bag.
3. Add the biscuits to the cinnamon and sugar and toss to coat the balls completely.
4. Lightly grease a mini loaf pan and layer the sugar coated biscuit balls into the pan.
5. Next, melt the butter in the microwave and then stir in the brown sugar. Pour over the top of the biscuits.
6. Bake for 7 minutes, turning the pan around about halfway through the cooking time.

Breakfast Burritos

This recipe is so foolproof, switch it up with your favorite proteins—bacon, leftover turkey, or tofu.

Prep time: 10 minutes
Cook time: 8 minutes
Serves: 2

Ingredients:
- 2 tortillas
- 4 eggs
- ½ cup sausage, cooked and cooled
- ½ red pepper, sliced into strips
- 1/3 cup mozzarella cheese
- ¼ cup salsa
- Salt and pepper to taste

Instructions:
1. Beat the eggs well with salt and pepper. The eggs can be either cooked in a nonstick pan in your air fryer for 5 minutes at 400 degrees, or scrambled on the stovetop in a pan.
2. Adjust temperature to 350 degrees.
3. Spoon the egg into the tortillas and add the red pepper, cheese, salsa and sausage (or desired protein). Don't overfill the tortillas.
4. Roll the tortillas tightly.
5. Line the air fryer rack with aluminum foil and put the rolled burritos on the foil. Spritz with oil.
6. Cook for 3 minutes and remove from the air fryer. Serve with additional salsa, sour cream or guacamole.

Air Fried Sausage

Don't forget to pierce the sausage skin to let out the steam; otherwise, your meat is liable to burst open.

Prep time: 1 minute
Cook time: 14 minutes
Serves: 2

Ingredients:
- 2-3 thick sausages

Instructions:
1. Preheat air fryer to 360 degrees.
2. Pierce the sausage skin with a fork.
3. Put the sausage in the air fryer and cook for 12 to 15 minutes. After about 6 minutes, give the fryer tray a good shake to prevent overcooking in any area.
4. Serve with eggs or cut up to use in another recipe.

Breakfast Soufflé

After trying this basic recipe, get creative and experiment with other ingredients, but be careful not to introduce too much moisture into the soufflé.

Prep time: 2 minutes
Cook time: 5-8 minutes
Serves: 2

Ingredients:
- 2 eggs
- 2 Tbsp. half and half
- Dried red chili pepper
- Salt and pepper to taste
- Dried parsley (optional)

Instructions:
1. Preheat the air fryer to 200 degrees. Combine all the ingredients, stirring well.
2. Lightly grease two soufflé dishes.
3. Place in the air fryer and cook for 5 minutes for a soft soufflé, or up to 8 minutes for a firmer soufflé.

Bagels

Daunted by all the steps of making bagels the old fashioned way? With the air fryer, you can skip so many steps, you'll wonder why you didn't try this before!

Prep time: 15 minutes
Cook time: 12 minutes
Serves: 2

Ingredients:
- ½ cup flour
- 1 tsp. baking powder
- 2 Tbsp. beaten egg white
- ½ cup Greek yogurt
- 1 tsp. sesame seeds

Instructions:
1. In a bowl, combine flour, a dash of salt and the baking powder. Combine thoroughly. Add Greek yogurt and mix with a fork until well combined. At this point, you will see pea-sized crumbles.
2. Dust your work surface with flour and kneed the dough until it's tacky but not overly sticky.
3. Preheat the air fryer to 325 degrees.
4. Divide in half and roll into balls. Then roll the balls into thick ropes, about ¾ inch thick. Join the ends to form the bagel shape.
5. Brush with egg white and sprinkle on the sesame seeds.
6. Add the bagels to the air fryer. Fry or 11 to 12 minutes, or until a nice golden brown.
7. Allow to cool slightly before cutting lengthwise and serving.

Ham and Egg Cups

Prep time: 15 minutes
Cook time: 15 minutes
Serves: 2

Ingredients:
- 2 eggs
- 4 slices of toast
- 1 slice of ham
- 2 Tbsp. butter, softened
- Salt and pepper to taste
- ¼ cup cheddar cheese

Instructions:
1. Preheat the air fryer to 160 degrees
2. Thoroughly coat the insides of two ramekins with butter.
3. Next, take the toast and flatten them as much as possible. Layer the edges of a ramekins with one piece of flattened bread. Repeat with the second ramekin. If necessary, trim some of the excess bread, but leave enough to create a good lip above the ramekin.
4. Repeat the process with the remaining flattened bread. Tuck the ham into the ramekins over the bread.
5. Crack an egg into each cup. Add a dash of salt and pepper, if desired, and top with the shredded cheese.
6. Carefully put the cups into the air fryer. Cook for 15 minutes.
7. When cooked, run a small knife around the inside of the ramekins, then gently coax out of the cups. Serve.

Donut Holes

These donuts are a great breakfast treat, and much healthier option than a traditional fried donut.

Prep time: 15 minutes
Cook time: 8 minutes
Serves: 2

Ingredients:
- 2 Tbsp. butter, chilled
- ½ cup sugar
- 1 Tbsp. whisked uncooked egg
- 2 cup flour
- 1 tsp. baking powder
- Dash of salt
- 2/3 cup plain yogurt
- ½ tsp. cinnamon

Instructions:
1. In a bowl, use a pastry cutter or your hands to combine the butter and about 1/3 cup of the sugar. Add the egg and mix well.
2. Next, mix together the salt, flour and baking powder. Add to the butter mixture and combine well.
3. Fold in the yogurt and mix until a good dough is created.
4. Roll into 9 to 10 balls, about 1 inch in diameter.
5. Preheat the air fryer to 360 degrees and grease the frying basket with oil. Add the donut holes and cook for about 4 minutes. Give the tray a shake and cook for another 4 minutes.
6. In the meantime, mix up the rest of the sugar with the cinnamon. When the donuts are baked thoroughly, remove them and roll them immediately in the cinnamon and sugar. Transfer to a baking rack and allow to cool for a few minutes (or as long as you can stand to wait!).

Appetizers

To many people, appetizers are even more fun than eating a main meal and will order straight from the first page of a menu in a restaurant.

It doesn't really matter if you want to use the following recipes a starting point in a meal, or as the main event—with the air fryer, you can indulge without the extra calories that load down a traditional oil-fried recipe.

Buffalo Fried Cauliflower

The kick of the buffalo sauce moderates the sweetness of the cauliflower very well. This recipe would also be great with broccoli.

Prep time: 10 minutes
Cook time: 17 minutes
Serves: 2

Ingredients:
- 2 cup cauliflower florets, raw
- ½ cup panko bread crumbs
- 1 tsp. sea salt
- 3 Tbsp. butter
- 3 Tbsp. buffalo sauce
- Ranch dressing for dipping

Instructions:
1. Melt the butter and whisk in buffalo sauce.
2. In a separate bowl, combine the bread crumbs with the salt.
3. Put each floret in the butter mixture, holding by the bottom of the stem. Allow the excess sauce to drip off.
4. Next, dredge the coated florets into the bread crumb mixture, coating well, and place in the air fryer basket. Repeat with remaining cauliflower.
5. Turn on the air fryer and adjust the temperature to 350 degrees. Cook for about 7 minutes and then give the fryer basket a good shake. Cook for another 7 to 10 minutes, shaking the basket periodically.
6. Remove from the air fryer and serve with ranch dressing or your favorite dipping sauce.

Air Fried Onion Rings

Prep time: 10 minutes + 1 hour to soak onions
Cook time: 8 minutes
Serves: 2

Ingredients:
- 2 onions
- 1 ¼ cup flour
- 1 ¼ cup milk
- 3 Tbsp. canola oil
- 1 egg
- 1 tsp. salt

Instructions:
1. Slice onions into even rings and soak in a bowl of ice water for 1 hour
2. Heat the air fryer to 350 degrees.
3. Whisk flour, milk, oil egg and salt together in a large bowl.
4. Remove onion rings from the water and pat dry with a paper towel. Dredge in the batter, evenly coating the rings.
5. Lightly spray the cooking basket with oil and add the battered onion rings. You may need to cook these in two batches so you don't overcrowd the onion rings in the air fryer.
6. Cook for 8 minutes, giving the frying basket a good shake after about 4 minutes.

Fried Mozzarella Sticks

If you don't want to use packaged string cheese, take a half pound of a block of mozzarella and cut into sticks.

Prep time: 5 minutes
Cook time: 8 minutes
Serves: 2

Ingredients:
- ½ package of mozzarella string cheese
- 2 eggs
- ¼ cup flour
- 1 cup panko bread crumbs
- ¼ cup milk

Instructions:
1. Combine egg and milk in a bowl and set aside. Put the bread crumbs in another bowl, and flour in a third bowl.
2. Remove string cheese from wrappers. Roll cheese in the flour, then dredge in the egg. Next, roll it in the bread crumbs.
3. Put on a cookie sheet lined with parchment paper and put in the freezer for 2 hours.
4. Heat the air fryer to 400 degrees.
5. Add about half of the cheese sticks to the fry basket and spritz with cooking oil. Fry for 12 minutes, giving the fry basket a good shake about halfway through. Repeat with remaining mozzarella sticks.

Fried Pickles

What air frying cookbook would be complete without a fried pickle recipe? For best results, use refrigerated pickles.

Prep time: 5 minutes
Cook time: 8 minutes
Serves: 2

Ingredients:
- 8 thick cut dill pickle slices
- 1/3 cup flour
- Pinch of baking powder
- 2 Tbsp. dark beer
- 2 Tbsp. water
- 1 Tbsp. cornstarch
- 4 Tbsp. panko bread crumbs
- Pinch of cayenne pepper
- Pinch of smoked paprika
- Ranch dressing for dipping

Instructions:
1. Carefully pat pickle slices dry and put aside.
2. In a bowl, mix together the beer, water, flour baking powder and a pinch of salt. The batter should resemble pancake batter. Add a little ore water if it's too thick. Set aside.
3. In a bowl, add the cornstarch. In a second bowl, mix together the panko bread crumbs with the paprika and cayenne pepper.
4. Preheat air fryer to 360 degrees and spritz the fryer basket with oil.
5. Press each pickle in the corn starch, then beer batter. Allow the excess batter to drip off and then dredge in the panko bread crumb mixture.
6. Place the battered pickles in the basket, but don't overcrowd. You may need to cook these in two batches.
7. Spritz the top of the pickles with additional cooking spray. Fry for 4 minutes. Flip over and spray top with oil. Cook for an additional 4 minutes, or until toasty golden brown.

Buffalo Wings

These wings are absolutely fantastic served with celery sticks and blue cheese or ranch dressing to dip in.

Prep time: 15 minutes + marinating time
Cook time: 12 minutes
Serves: 2

Ingredients:
- 1 lb. chicken wings
- 4 Tbsp. butter, separated
- 4 Tbsp. Frank's hot sauce, separated

Instructions:
1. Remove wing tips and discard. Rinse and pat dry with paper towels. Set aside.
2. Combine 2 Tbsp. of melted butter and 2 Tbsp. of hot sauce. Place in plastic storage bag and add the chicken wings. Seal and shake to coat the wings.
3. Marinate for a least 2 hours, or overnight if preferred.
4. When marinating time has been reached, remove the chicken wings from the refrigerator and allow to come to room temperature.
5. In the meantime, preheat the air fryer to 400 degrees.
6. Add the wings to the fryer basket and cook for six minutes. Shake the basket well and cook for another six minutes.
7. While the wings are cooking, create the sauce by melting the rest of the butter and combining with the remaining hot sauce. Put aside.
8. When the wings are ready, remove from the air fryer and toss with the newly prepared sauce and serve.

Jalapeno Poppers

When you're cutting these peppers in half, try to keep the halves together since you'll be rejoining them after they are stuffed.

Prep time: 20 minutes
Cook time: 10 minutes
Serves: 2

Ingredients:
- 4 jalapeno peppers, sliced lengthwise with the seeds and stems removed
- 2 spring roll wrappers
- ¼ cup cheddar cheese
- 2 Tbsp. raw egg, beaten

Instructions:
1. Cut the spring roll wrappers in half. Brush each half with some egg wash.
2. Slice the cheese into thin strips and place in one jalapeno half, covering it with the other half. Place the jalapeno in one corner of the spring roll wrapper and roll the pepper tightly, sealing the edges tightly.
3. Brush the outside of the rolled pepper with the egg and spritz with cooking spray.
4. Add the jalapeno poppers to the air fryer basket.
5. Turn your air fryer on and set the temperature to 370 degrees. Cook for about 8 to 10 minutes.
6. Serve with marinara sauce.

Potato Chips

These are so delicious you'll never want to eat another bagged chip again!

Prep time: 15 minutes
Cook time: 30 minutes
Serves: 2

Ingredients:
- 3 russet potatoes
- 1 Tbsp. duck fat or ghee
- Sea salt to taste

Instructions:
1. Peel the potatoes. With a mandolin or a very sharp knife, slice the potatoes into very thin slices.
2. Place the sliced potatoes in a bath of cold water. Let soak for a few minutes, then drain and carefully dry the potatoes.
3. Melt the duck fat or ghee and rub onto the potato slices.
4. Add the slices to the air fryer basket. You can layer them, but be prepared to make them in two batches so you don't go over 4 layers deep.
5. Fry the chips at 170 degrees for about 20 minutes, giving the basket a good shake and flip around the potato slices every 5 minutes or so to evenly cook them.
6. After they are dry to the touch, increase the temperature to 400 degrees to finish off the crisping process.
7. Remove from heat and toss with salt. Serve.

Fried Vegetable Tots

These vegetable tots are so yummy that even the pickiest eaters will be coming back for more.

Prep time: 10 minutes
Cook time: 10 minutes
Serves: 2

Ingredients:
- ½ zucchini
- 1 carrot
- 1 egg
- 2 Tbsp. bread crumbs
- 2 Tbsp. Parmesan cheese
- Salt and pepper to taste

Instructions:
1. Heat air fryer to 400 degrees.
2. Peel and grate the zucchini and carrot. With a clean dish towel or cheese cloth, squeeze out the excess liquid.
3. In a bowl, combine the zucchini and carrot with the remaining ingredients.
4. Roll them into the traditional 'tot' form and add to the fryer basket. Spritz with a little cooking spray, if desired.
5. Bake for about 5 minutes. Give the fryer basket a good shake and cook for about 5 more minutes until golden brown.

Blooming Onion Blossom

This serves two but it is so good and much healthier than the traditional blooming onion that you might not want to share!

Prep time: 15 minutes + 3 hours for an ice bath
Cook time: 20 minutes
Serves: 2

Ingredients:
- 1 Vidalia onion
- 1/3 cup milk
- 2 eggs
- ¾ cup panko bread crumbs
- 1 tsp. garlic salt
- 1 tsp. paprika
- ½ tsp. oregano
- 1/8 tsp. cayenne pepper
- Dash of vegetable oil

Instructions:
1. First, peel the onion. Cut off one end and then make about 10 to 12 slices around the perimeter of the onion (making sure not to cut through to the bottom). Open the 'petals' and then cut out the very center of the onion.
2. Soak the onion in ice water for 2 to3 hours.
3. In the meantime, combine the bread crumbs and the spices, mixing well.
4. In another bowl, mix together the eggs and milk.
5. When the onion is ready, remove from the ice bath and dry well. Put it on a plate and coat with the onion and milk mixture.
6. Pat the breadcrumb mixture onto the onion petals and place in air fryer. Spritz with cooking oil.
7. Turn on the air fryer and set the temperature to 400 degrees. After 10 minutes, check the onion for doneness. If it's not done and the edges of the onion are turning too brown, you can tent it with aluminum foil to prevent overbrowning.
8. Fry for an additional 5 to 10 minutes, depending on how large the onion is.
9. When ready, remove from the air fryer and serve hot with your favorite dipping sauce.

Curly Fries

These curly shapes are so fun, you can't eat them without a smile on your face. This recipe also works well for sweet potatoes.

Prep time: 5 minutes
Cook time: 15 minutes
Serves: 2

Ingredients:
- 1 large potato
- 1 Tbsp. coconut oil
- 1 Tbsp. olive oil
- Salt and pepper to taste
- Ketchup or melted cheese to dip in

Instructions:
1. Peel potato and use a spiralizer to make them into curly fry shapes.
2. Preheat air fryer to 350 degrees.
3. In a bowl, combine the olive oil and coconut oil. Dredge the curly fries in the oil mixture.
4. Put them in the air fryer and cook for about 15 minutes or until desired doneness.
5. Remove from the air fryer and sprinkle with salt and pepper. Serve with ketchup or your favorite melted cheese to dunk in.

Garlic Bread and Cheese

If you want to dress this dish up even more, add 1 teaspoon of pesto or sun-dried tomato pesto on top of the butter layer.

Prep time: 5 minutes
Cook time: 6 minutes
Serves: 2

Ingredients:
- Italian bread cut into 4 slices
- 3 Tbsp. butter, softened but not melted
- 2 garlic cloves
- 2/3 cup mozzarella cheese, grated

Instructions:
1. Mince garlic and add to the butter ahead of time to allow the flavors to meld.
2. Heat air fryer to 350 degrees.
3. Spread the butter on the slices of bread and top each slice with the grated mozzarella cheese.
4. Place the bread in the air fryer and cook for about 6 minutes, or until the cheese is thoroughly melted.
5. Enjoy as an appetizer or as a side to your favorite pasta dish.

Fried Zucchini Spears

When slicing these, the thinner the slices, the quicker they are going to cook.

Prep time: 10 minutes
Cook time: 35 minutes
Serves: 2

Ingredients:
- 1 zucchini
- 1 egg white, whipped
- 1/3 cup panko bread crumbs
- 3 Tbsp. Parmesan cheese
- 1/8 tsp. oregano
- 1/8 tsp. cayenne pepper
- 1/8 tsp. dried basil

Instructions:
1. Combine the panko bread crumbs, cheese and herbs, along with salt and pepper to taste. Set aside.
2. Wash the zucchini and dry well, but do not peel it. Slice the zucchini in half and then cut into wedges about ½ inch thick, but no ticker.
3. Heat the air fryer to 390 degrees.
4. Put the egg white in a bowl and the bread crumbs in another bowl.
5. Dip zucchini wedges in the egg white, and then in the bread crumb mixture to coat it.
6. Place in a greased frying basket. Cook breaded zucchini for about 7 minutes, and then carefully turn them over, cooking for an additional 7 minutes.
7. These are delicious served with bleu cheese or ranch dressing.

Coconut Shrimp

If you want to give this an extra kick, mix in about ¼ teaspoon of hot sauce to the marmalade dipping sauce when serving.

Prep time: 10 minutes
Cook time: 20 minutes
Serves: 2

Ingredients:
- 10 large shrimp, deveined and with shells removed
- 1 cup coconut milk
- 2/3 cup shredded coconut
- 1/3 cup panko bread crumbs
- ½ tsp. cayenne pepper
- Salt and pepper to taste
- 1/3 cup orange marmalade
- 2 Tbsp. honey

Instructions:
1. Rinse and pat the shrimp dry with a paper towel. Set aside.
2. In a small bowl, combine the coconut milk with a little salt and pepper. Set aside. In a separate small bowl, combine the coconut, panko bread crumbs, cayenne pepper and salt and pepper to taste.
3. Heat the air fryer to 350 degrees.
4. Dip the shrimp in coconut milk, then dredge in the bread crumb mixture. Add to the fryer basket, repeating until all 10 shrimp are ready to cook.
5. Cook for about 10 minutes. Then give the basket a good shake and cook for another 10 minutes.
6. While the shrimp are cooking, combine the marmalade and honey. Put it in a bowl to use as the dipping sauce.
7. When the shrimp is ready, serve immediately.

Desserts

What can you make for dessert using your air fryer? A LOT! There are some fantastic recipes that have either been created specifically for the appliance, or modified to complement this cooking method.

Whether you have a hankering for pie or cookies… or even chocolate cake… your new best kitchen friend is sitting there, ready to help you bake up the perfect end to any meal.

Chocolate Cake

Who says you can't have your cake—and your air fryer—and eat it too? (The cake, not the appliance.)

Prep time: 10 minutes
Cook time: 25 minutes
Serves: 2

Ingredients:
- 1 cup white flour
- 3 medium eggs
- 2/3 cup sour cream
- 6 Tbsp. butter
- 2/3 cup white sugar
- ¼ cup cocoa powder
- 1 tsp. baking powder
- ½ tsp. baking soda
- 1 ½ tsp. vanilla
- Your favorite frosting

Instructions:
1. Heat air fryer to 160 degrees.
2. Combine the flour, sugar, cocoa powder, baking soda and baking powder. Set aside.
3. In a mixing bowl, cream together the add the sour cream, butter, eggs and vanilla. Add dry ingredients and mix well.
4. Prepare the baking tray by spraying it and lightly dusting it with flour. Pour the batter into the baking tray and set in the air fryer.
5. Bake for 25 minutes.

6. Check for doneness by inserting a toothpick in the center. If it comes out clean, the cake is ready. If batter clings to the toothpick, bake for an additional 2 to 4 minutes.
7. When ready, cook the cake on a wire rack. When completely cool, top with your favorite frosting and serve.

Funnel Cake Bites

Now you don't have to wait until your local carnival or fair comes to town—make these funnel cake bites anytime.

Prep time: 8 minutes
Cook time: 8 minutes
Serves: 2

Ingredients:
- 2/3 cup Greek yogurt
- 2/3 cup self rising flour, separated
- ½ tsp. vanilla
- Powdered sugar or apple pie filling

Instructions:
1. Preheat air fryer to 375 degrees.
2. Combine the yogurt, vanilla and about ½ flour, reserving the remaining flour to roll the dough.
3. Roll dough and cut into bite sized squares.
4. Lightly spritz the fryer basket with oil and add 8 funnel cake bites at a time.
5. Cook for about 4 minutes, then flip and cook for an additional 3 to 4 minutes.
6. Repeat with remaining dough.
7. Lightly dust finished cake bites with powdered sugar, or serve with warm apple pie filling to dip in.

Fried Apple Pie

After you master these mini apple pies, switch it up with other pie fillings.

Prep time: 15 minutes
Cook time: 6 minutes
Serves: 2

Ingredients:
- Refrigerated pie crust
- 4 utility apples
- 1 tsp. flour
- ¼ tsp. cinnamon
- 2 Tbsp. sugar
- 1 raw egg, beaten
- 2 tsp. sugar

Instructions:
1. Prepare 4 ramekins. Cut four circles from the pie crust to line each ramekin.
2. Peel and thinly slice the apples. Mix with the flour, cinnamon and 2 Tbsp of sugar. Add the filling to the lined ramekins and cut out four smaller circles to top the ramekins.
3. Seal the apple pies and cut slits into the top crusts to allow steam to escape. Brush tops with egg wash and sprinkle the 2 teaspoons of sugar on the top.
4. Add the ramekins to the air fryer.
5. Turn on air fryer and set the temperature to 360 degrees.
6. Bake for 6 minutes. Check the pies. You should be able to see some filling bubbling through the slits in the tops of the crust. If not, bake for an additional 3 to 4 minutes, or until done.

Crustless Coconut pie

Prep time: 7 minutes
Cook time: 12 minutes
Serves: 2

Ingredients:
- 1 egg
- 1 cup milk
- 2 Tbsp. butter
- ½ tsp. vanilla extract
- ¼ cup sugar
- ¼ cup coconut flour
- 1 Tbsp. coconut oil
- 2 Tbsp. toasted coconut

Instructions:
1. In a mixing bowl, combine all the ingredients. Stir until well blended, but don't over-stir.
2. Coat two ramekins lightly with coconut oil and pour batter into the ramekins.
3. Heat air fryer to 350 degrees. Add the ramekins to the air basket and cook for about 10 to 12 minutes, checking to make sure it's baking evenly.
4. Allow to cool slightly, top with toasted coconut and serve.

Apple Chips

These apple chips are extremely portable, so double the recipe and take some to work the next day for a guilt-free snack.

Prep time: 7 minutes
Cook time: 12 minutes
Serves: 2

Ingredients:
- 2 utility apples, such as Macintosh apples
- ½ tsp. cinnamon
- ½ tsp. nutmeg
- 1 tsp. sugar

Instructions:
1. Heat air fryer to 375 degrees.
2. Core apples and thinly slice the apples. Mix cinnamon and nutmeg with the sugar in a bowl, then toss apple slices in the mixture.
3. Bake for 4 minutes, then flip and bake for an additional 4 minutes.

Fruity Mug Cakes

This versatile recipe loves any combination of fruit, such as strawberries and rhubarb.

Prep time: 5 minutes
Cook time: 15 minutes
Serves: 2

Ingredients:

- ¼ cup flour
- 2 Tbsp. butter
- 1 Tbsp. sugar
- 1 Tbsp. brown sugar
- 1 Tbsp. oatmeal
- 2 plums
- 1 peach
- 1 apple
- 2 tsp. honey

Instructions:

1. Heat air fryer to 325 degrees
2. Remove seeds from the apple and the stones from the plums and peach. Dice fruit into small pieces.
3. Lightly coat two mugs with cooking spray. Divide fruit between the mugs. Top with brown sugar and honey. Set aside.
4. In a bowl, combine flour, butter and white sugar. When it resembles pea sized crumbs, add the oats and mix well. Top fruit with the oat mixture.
5. Place mugs in the air fryer and bake for 10 minutes. Then increase the temperature to 400 degrees and cook for an additional 4 to 5 minutes, or until the crumble is nicely browned.

Rainbow Donuts

These donuts are sure to brighten up the stormiest of days.

Prep time: 15 minutes
Cook time: 5 minutes
Serves: 2

Ingredients:
- 2 Pillsbury Grands biscuits
- ½ cup powdered sugar
- 1-2 Tbsp. milk
- 1/8 tsp. vanilla
- 2/3 cup shredded coconut
- 1 cup Fruity Pebbles cereal, divided into color families
- 1 butterscotch candy, crushed into small pieces

Instructions:
1. Use a biscuit cutter to cut 1 inch circles in the holes of each biscuit. Do not flatten the biscuits.
2. Lightly grease the basket of your air fryer and set the temperature for 350 degrees. Add the donuts and cook for five minutes.
3. In the meantime, combine powdered sugar, milk and vanilla.
4. Remove donuts and allow to cool.
5. Dip the top of each donut into the icing to coat the top. Place donuts on a plate, icing side up. Before the icing dries, press shredded coconut into the bottom of the donut. Sprinkle some of the butterscotch candy in the coconut to make it look like gold pieces.
6. Press a red line of cereal across the top of the donut. Repeat with a line of orange cereal, and hen yellow, green, blue and purple so it forms a complete rainbow.
7. Let the frosting harden completely and serve.

Lemon Pound Cake

This tangy sweet cake can easily be tripled and made into a cake for a full family. Adjust baking time accordingly.

Prep time: 10 minutes
Cook time: 5 minutes
Serves: 2

Ingredients:
- 3 Tbsp. flour
- 1/8 tsp. baking powder
- Dash of salt
- 2 Tbsp. butter, softened
- 1/3 cup sugar
- 1/3 cup powdered sugar
- 2 tsp. lemon juice
- 1 egg
- ½ tsp. vanilla
- ½ tsp. lemon juice

Instructions:
1. Prepare two ramekins by lightly greasing them.
2. In a bowl, combine flour, baking powder and salt. Mix well.
3. In a mixing bowl, cream together the butter, and the granulated sugar. Add the two teaspoons of lemon juice, egg and vanilla. Add the flour mixture slowly.
4. Divide the batter between the two ramekins.
5. Heat air fryer to 330 degrees.
6. Place ramekins in the air fryer and bake for about 20 to 25 minutes or until a toothpick inserted in the middle of the cakes comes out clean.
7. When the cakes are done remove and allow to cool for about 15 minutes.
8. Create the glaze by stirring the powdered sugar with the ½ tsp. of lemon juice. Drizzle over the cakes and serve.

Apple Dumplings

As with many other air fryer recipes, it's very important to make sure to turn the apples over halfway through the cooking time. Otherwise, the both the pastry and apple will be cooked unevenly.

Prep time: 10minutes
Cook time: 25 minutes
Serves: 2

Ingredients:
- 2 utility apples, like Macintosh apples
- 2 sheets of puffed pastry
- 3 Tbsp. brown raisins
- 1 Tbsp. light brown sugar
- ½ tsp. cinnamon
- 2 Tbsp. butter

Instructions:
1. Heat air fryer to 355 degrees.
2. Peel your apples and remove the cores. Keep the apples whole, and do not slice into segments.
3. In a bowl, combine the raisins, brown sugar and cinnamon. Put the raisin mixture in the center of the apples. Set the apples on the puffed pastry sheets and wrap around the apple, sealing the pastry well around the apple.
4. Melt the butter and brush the outside of the pastry.
5. Spritz the bottom of your frying basket with oil and add the apples.
6. Cook for about 12 to 13 minutes, then open the fryer and turn the apples over. Cook for an additional 12 minutes.
7. Remove and allow to cool for about 8 to 10 minutes before serving.

Chocolate Soufflé

This decadent dessert for two is the perfect way to end a date night dinner.

Prep time: 15 minutes
Cook time: 15 minutes
Serves: 2

Ingredients:
- 1/3 cup butter, softened
- 3 oz. baking chocolate, chopped
- 2 Tbsp. flour
- 2 large eggs, separated
- 3 Tbsp. granulated sugar
- ½ tsp. vanilla
- ½ cup whipping cream
- 3 Tbsp. sugar

Instructions:
1. Lightly grease two ramekins with butter and coat with sugar. Set aside.
2. Using a double boiler, melt he chocolate and butter together, stirring until mixed well.
3. In another bowl, beat the two egg yolks. Add to sugar and vanilla and combine thoroughly. Add the chocolate and butter mixture, stirring well to incorporate thoroughly. Stir in the flour, mixing until the batter has no lumps.
4. Pre heat the air fryer to 330 degrees.
5. In another bowl, whisk the egg whites until they are starting to show peaks. Fold half of the egg whites to the chocolate mixture, then fold in remaining whites.
6. Carefully spoon batter into the ramekins, allowing about ½ inch at the top.
7. Place ramekins in the air fryer. Bake for 15 minutes.
8. In the meantime, whip the whipped cream and sugar. Set aside.
9. When the soufflé is cool, top with a dollop of whipped cream.

Caramel Cheesecake

Prep time: 20 minutes
Cook time: 40 minutes
Serves: 2

Ingredients:
- 1 can sweetened condensed milk
- 3 Tbsp. butter, melted
- 1/3 cup graham cracker crumbs
- 2 cup cream cheese
- 1 cup sugar
- 4 eggs
- 1 Tbsp. pure vanilla extract

Instructions:
1. Heat sweetened condensed milk in its can in a pot of water over low heat for about 40 minutes.
2. Heat air fryer to 350 degrees.
3. Prepare a small spring form pan by lightly greasing and dusting with flour. Combine graham crackers with the butter and press into the bottom of the pan.
4. Combine sugar and cream cheese with a mixer until it's creamy. Add eggs and vanilla, blending well. Set aside. Open the sweetened condensed milk—now a creamy caramel consistency—add to the cream cheese mixture. Pour entire batter into the spring form pan.
5. Cook for 15 minutes, then reduce the air fryer to 325 degrees and bake for 10 more minutes. Then reduce the temperature to 300 degrees and bake for 15 more minutes.
6. Allow to cool for at least 6 hours to overnight. If desired, top with melted chocolate.

Lemony Cupcakes

This recipe allows for two cupcakes to share after dinner, with two more for the morning... if you can wait that long!

Prep time: 15 minutes
Cook time: 8 minutes
Serves: 2

Ingredients:
- ½ cup butter
- ½ cup self-rising flour
- ½ cup sugar
- 1 egg white
- 1/8 tsp. vanilla

For the icing:
- ¼ cup powdered sugar
- 2 tsp. lemon juice
- ½ tsp. lemon zest

Instructions:
1. Preheat air fryer to 340 degrees.
2. In a mixing bowl, cream butter, sugar and vanilla until the mixture is light and fluffy. Beat in the egg and 3 tablespoons of flour. Gently fold in remaining flour.
3. Prepare 4 silicone muffin cups by spraying lightly with cooking oil. Add the batter and put the cupcakes in the air fryer. Bake for 8 minutes.
4. Remove from the air fryer when fully baked and put on a cooling rack to cool.
5. In the meantime, mix powered sugar, lemon juice and lemon zest. Drizzle over the cooled cakes and serve.

Mince Pies

It's tempting to put extra mincemeat in these pies, but make sure you don't overfill them or the filling might boil over and made a huge mess.

Prep time: 10 minutes
Cook time: 12 minutes
Serves: 2

Ingredients:
- ½ cup flour
- Half stick butter
- 2 tsp. sugar
- ½ cup jar mincemeat
- 1 egg white, beaten

Instructions:
1. Heat the air fryer to 350 degrees.
2. Combine flour and butter until it resembles tiny pea shaped crumbs. Add sugar and mix well.
3. Roll out the dough, and add to your mini pie pans.
4. Fill each with ¼ cup of mincemeat and top with another circle of pastry.
5. Slit the top with a knife to allow for steam to escape and brush with egg bath.
6. Place pies in the air fryer and cook for 12 minutes.

Banana Bread

Banana bread is delicious right out of the oven, or toasted slightly in the morning for breakfast.

Prep time: 10 minutes
Cook time: 25 minutes
Serves: 2

Ingredients:
- ½ cup self rising flour
- 1/8 tsp. baking soda
- 1/3 cup bananas, mashed
- ½ cup sugar
- 3 Tbsp. butter
- 1 egg

Instructions:
1. Grease your mini loaf baking pan ad preheat the air fryer to 350 degrees
2. Combine flour with baking soda, set aside.
3. In a mixing bowl, cream the butter and sugar, then add mashed bananas. Add ½ of the flour mixture, then the egg. Stir in remaining flour.
4. Put the batter in the prepared loaf and bake for 10 minutes. Reduce the temperature to 335 degrees and bake for an additional 15 minutes.

Chocolate Chip Cookies a la Air Fryer

These cookies are so easy to make in the air fryer, you'll be making a batch every day, even in the warmest months when you don't want to turn the oven on!

Prep time: 5 minutes
Cook time: 15 minutes
Serves: 2

Ingredients:
- 1 ¼ cup self rising flour
- 3 Tbsp. sugar
- 5 Tbsp. brown sugar
- ¾ cup butter
- ½ cup chocolate chips
- ¼ cup honey
- 1 Tbsp. milk
- 1 Tbsp. cocoa powder
- 1 tsp. vanilla

Instructions:
1. Preheat the air fryer to 350 degrees
2. Cream butter and sugars together in a mixing bowl until light and fluffy. Add all of the remaining ingredients except for the chocolate chips. Mix well. Fold in chocolate chips.
3. Roll batter into 12 even balls.
4. Cover the air fryer tray with aluminum foil. Place cookie balls on the sheet.
5. Bake for 15 minutes.
6. Allow to cool about 5 minutes after baking before transferring to a cooling rack to complete the cooling process.

Banana S'mores

Prep time: 5 minutes
Cook time: 15 minutes
Serves: 2

Ingredients:
- 2 bananas
- 2 Tbsp. chocolate chips
- 1 Tbsp. peanut butter chips
- 4 tsp. mini marshmallows
- 2 tsp. graham cracker cereal

Instructions:
1. Preheat the air fryer to 400 degrees.
2. Slice unpeeled bananas on the inside of the banana, being careful not to slice through the other side. Pull the peelings open slightly to firm a pocket.
3. Fill the banana pocket with the chips and marshmallows. Next, add a few pieces of graham cracker cereal into the chips and marshmallows.
4. Carefully place bananas in the fryer basket, tipping the bananas toward each other to keep upright. Fry for about 6 minutes. The peel will have turned black, but the inner banana will be soft and the marshmallows will have melted.
5. Remove from the air fryer and allow to cool for a few minutes. To serve, scoop out the filling and plate.

Conclusion

We are so glad you took the leap to this healthier cooking format with us!

The air fryer truly isn't a gadget that should stay on the shelf. Instead, take it out and give it a whirl when you're whipping up one of your tried-and-true recipes, or if you're just starting to get your feet wet with the air frying method.

Regardless of appliances, recipes or dietary concerns, we hope you have fun in your kitchen. Between food prep, cooking time and then the (dreaded) cleanup, a lot of time is spent in this one room, so it should be as fun as possible.

Thank you for taking the time to pursue the Air Fryer Cookbook For Two. Happy, healthy eating!

Made in the USA
Coppell, TX
05 November 2024

39681714R00077